REUTERS GLOSSARY

REUTERS GLOSSARY:
INTERNATIONAL ECONOMIC &
FINANCIAL TERMS

Edited by
the senior staff of Reuters Limited

Longman 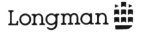   REUTERS

REUTERS GLOSSARY:
INTERNATIONAL ECONOMIC & FINANCIAL TERMS

Published by Longman Group UK Limited, Westgate House, The High, Harlow, Essex,
CM20 1YR, United Kingdom.
Telephone (0279) 442601
Telex 817484
Facsimile (0279) 444501

ISBN 0 582 04286 0

British Library Cataloguing in Publication Data
Reuters glossary: international economic & financial terms.
　1. Economics — Encyclopaedias
　330′.03′21

ISBN 0–582–04286–0

Printed and bound in Great Britain by
Mackays of Chatham PLC

Foreword

Reuters is the world's leading supplier of business and economic news and information to the professional financial community and to the media. Reuters staff of over 1,100 journalists produces news services which are distributed in more than 150 countries. Reuters reference book on economic and financial terms, originally compiled for its own staff, was published in 1982 in response to enquiries from subscribers for a guide to the technical terms used in its specialised business services. This latest volume has been reorganised into seven separate sections for ease of reference. The Reuters Glossary now contains additional definitions dealing with the international capital markets, financial futures and energy. It is intended for use by Reuters staff, its subscribers and the many others who we believe will find the information of value.

I should like to thank those individuals and organisations who helped in the compilation of this book.

November 1988

Glen Renfrew
Managing Director

Organisation

This book is a comprehensive revision of the Reuters Glossary of International Economic and Financial Terms published in 1982.

The entries are split into seven sections relating to the markets in which Reuters specialist business journalists operate. The aim is to provide a quick overview of each field. Sections such as "Equities" and "Energy" are self-explanatory but as currency specialists also deal with wider economic topics, the "Economy, Currency" section includes general economic terms, as well as those dealing with foreign exchange and international institutions. "Lending" embraces both money and capital markets.

Each section is presented in alphabetical order. Readers looking for individual terms may find it easier to consult the cross-referenced A-Z index and the list of Abbreviations and Acronyms at the end of the volume.

Headings, written in bold face, are given in full and followed, where appropriate, by an abbreviation. Example: **Bank For International Settlements (BIS)**. The definition may be found in the "Economy, Currency" section as well as in the A-Z index, or through the Abbreviation and Acronyms list by looking up BIS.

There are cross-references for entries occurring either in the same section or in another category. Examples: in the sector "Economy, Currency", the entry for **Barter** concludes with "See **Compensation Trade, Counter-Trade**," which points to new terms occurring within the same sector. The entry **Baltic Futures Exchange (BFE)** in "Commodities" concludes with "See entry **Baltic Exchange** under SHIPPING," indicating that the new term appears in the "Shipping" section.

No all-in-one glossary can be as comprehensive as existing reference works devoted to individual markets. In meeting the needs of Reuter journalists, we hope to assist a wider readership in the economic and financial fields concerned.

Senior executives of the following organisations read the manuscript of the earlier Reuters Glossary and offered suggestions which were incorporated in it:

London Commodity Exchange Co. Ltd., Asian Development Bank, Grain & Feed Trade Association Ltd., London Metal Exchange, New York Stock Exchange, Chemical Bank, Goldman Sachs & Co., Commodity Exchange Inc., Securities Industry Association, Chicago Board of Trade, American Institute of Certified Public Accountants.

Responsibility for the contents of this Glossary rests entirely with Reuters.

Colin Mooney
Reuters International Quality Editor

Contents

General Market Terms

After Hours Trading
Trading based on rules and terms of an equity, futures or terminal market after the official close of the market.

All Or None
Market or limited price order requiring that no part of an order be executed unless all of it can be executed at the specified price.

Alternative Order
Order to do either of two alternatives, e.g. either sell or buy a particular stock at a limit price.

Arbitrage
Simultaneous purchase of foreign exchange, securities, financial instruments or commodities in one market and sale in another (at a higher price) or the simultaneous matching of trades in one commodity on two markets, or a profitable spot or forward exchange transaction to exploit yield differentials in different centres. See **Risk Arbitrageurs** under EQUITIES.

Asked Price
Price at which a security or commodity is offered for sale or the rate at which a loan is offered. Market participants bid to buy and offer to sell. See **Bid** and **Offer**.

At Best
Instruction with a buying or selling order indicating it should be carried out immediately at the best possible price. Also known as **At The Market**. See **Limit Order, Market Order, Stop Order** and **Time Order**.

At Or Better
Instruction to trade at a specific level or better.

At Par
Nominal or face value of a security.

At The Close
Market order to be executed as near to the close as possible.

At The Market
See **At Best**.

At-The-Money
An option with an exercise price equal to or near the current price of the underlying instrument. See **Call Option, Exercise Price, In-The-Money, Option, Out-Of-The-Money** and **Put Option**.

At The Opening
Market order to be executed at the opening or not at all.

Averaging
Purchases or sales of shares, stocks or commodities at different prices, thus adjusting the average price; it can also mean making regular purchases through investing a fixed amount in a security etc., with the amount of stock received depending on the price level (known as dollar cost averaging in the USA).

Away US term for trade, quote or market that does not approximate to current market levels.

Back And Filling Numerous small rises and falls in a (usually speculative) market, but without any overall major change in price levels.

Basis Point Unit of measure (usually one hundredth of a percentage point, i.e. 0.01 per cent) used to express movements in interest rates, foreign exchange rates or bond yields. See entry under LENDING.

Bear Investor who sells short in the expectation of a decline in a currency, the price of a commodity, stock, bond etc. with the hope of buying back at a lower price. If he sells something he does not have, he is called an uncovered bear in the UK, shortseller in the USA. Bear often describes an investor who just believes a specific market is going down. Opposite to **Bull**.

Bear Covering Situation where bears who have previously sold a currency, commodity or stock etc. are now buying them again, i.e. covering themselves. Short covering means the same. See **Short Covering**.

Bear Market Market in which prices are declining, or in which participants expect price declines. Opposite to **Bull Market**.

Bear Raid Heavy shortselling by one or more big traders hoping to depress prices so that they can profitably repurchase at lower rates.

Bear Squeeze Strategy whereby central banks support a currency in order to pressure speculators holding uncovered short positions. In a successful bear squeeze, the shorts have to buy back at a higher price than they sold for. Can also occur in other markets, though without official action, e.g. commodity markets.

Best Effort US term for a new securities issue which is not underwritten or purchased as a whole but sold on the basis of what can be sold. It can also mean an order to sell currency or securities at the best available price over a given period.

Bid Undertaking to buy a commodity, security, currency or any instrument at a specified price; the price a purchaser is willing to pay. See **Asked Price** and **Offer**.

Bid And Asked Highest price a dealer has said he is prepared to pay for a security or commodity at a specific time. The asked price is the lowest that anyone will accept at the same time.

Bid Market Market where bids predominate over offers at the ruling market price. Opposite to **Offered Market**.

Board Order Order to buy (or sell) when a particular price is reached.

Break A rapid and sharp price decline.

Breakout The rise or fall in a market price beyond a level where it had previously halted.

Broad Tape US term for news wires carrying prices and information on securities and commodities as opposed to the narrower (price) tape used by the exchanges.

Broker An individual or company that matches bids and offers in a market and charges a commission fee. See entry under EQUITIES.

Brokerage Fee or commission charged by a broker. In the USA, it is also commonly used to refer to a brokerage firm.

Broker's Line Direct telephone line between a broker and a customer.

Bucket Shop Unlawful or doubtful organisation dealing unscrupulously in commodities or stocks. In the UK the term is most frequently used to describe travel agents selling cheap airline tickets.

Bull Investor who buys in the expectation of a rise in the price of a stock, commodity, currency etc. Often describes someone who just believes a specific market is rising. Opposite to **Bear**.

Bull Market Market in which prices are rising, or in which participants expect higher prices. Opposite to **Bear Market**.

Buoyant Description of a market where prices rise easily with underlying strong tone.

Buy At Best To bid higher and higher prices without any limit until the required quantity is purchased.

Buy In To close out a short position. See **Bear Covering** and **Short Covering**. Compare **Buying In** under EQUITIES.

Buy/Sell On Close US term for purchases/sales at the end of the trading session within the closing range.

Buy/Sell On Opening US term for purchases/sales at the start of the trading session within the opening range.

Buyer's Market One in which producers are willing to produce, or sellers willing to market, larger amounts than buyers are currently willing to buy at existing prices. This usually results in marked price declines. See **Seller's Market**.

Buyer's Option Allows a buyer to settle a forward contract at his option within a set period. In commodities he can decide between a choice of delivery dates or commodities of the same grade from different origins.

Buyer's Over Price which is still valid after trading ends, if buying orders are unfulfilled.

Buying In If a seller of stocks fails to deliver them within the set time, the buyer may buy them in where he can and any additional costs and expenses are chargeable to the seller.

Call (Session) Trading period during which the price for each future contract is established, i.e. opening, midsession or closing calls. See entry under EQUITIES.

Call Option Option or contract giving the holder the right to buy a certain amount e.g. of stock or commodity futures at a specified price at a specified forward date, or within a specified period. In the Eurobond market, a call option allows a borrower to redeem a bond before its final maturity, normally at a small premium to the issue price.

Call Purchase Transaction in which the seller has some option of pricing at a later date within a given range of the existing price. See **Call Sale** and **Fixation**.

Call Rule Official bid price established competitively at the close of each day's trading and valid until the exchange reopens.

Call Sale Transaction in which the purchaser has some option of pricing at a later date within a given range of the existing price. See **Call Purchase** and **Fixation**.

Carry Cost of financing, i.e. borrowing to purchase, a position in financial instruments. When the short term interest rate is greater than the current return on the instrument, the carry is a negative one. If the financing cost is less than the return, it is a positive carry.

Charting Use of graphs and charts in the technical analysis of markets to plot and forecast trends. Price movements and average price movements are often part of charting. The chartists, or technical analysts, believe they can see recurring patterns on charts which enable them to predict future price movements and so put them in a position to make sound buy or sell recommendations to clients. See **Fundamental Analysis** and **Technical Analysis**.

Examples of chart patterns are:
Ascending tops. During a lengthy price rise each peak is higher than the preceding peak, indicating an upward trend is still likely.
Descending tops. Here each new high is lower than the pattern's previous high, meaning the outlook is bearish.
Flag. This pattern, with flagpoles on either side, contains a price consolidation. An upward movement before the consolidation points to further gains, a decline before the pattern is seen as evidence of a fresh fall.
Head and shoulders. Lines are drawn on the chart to reveal a head and shoulders shape. Chartists conclude this means a trend is being reversed.
Rising bottoms. Study of the chart shows a rising trend in price "lows", meaning higher basic support levels for that price.

Churning

Excessive trading which permits a broker who controls an account to earn extra commissions while disregarding the best interests of the customer.

CIF

Cost, insurance and freight. A CIF shipping price means that it includes the cost of goods, their insurance and freight. The purchaser of CIF goods bears no expenses until he takes the goods from the ship or plane at destination. Due fulfilment by the seller may take place when he passes to the buyer the invoice, the insurance policy and bill of lading. See **FOB** and **FAS**.

Clearing

Procedure through which a clearing house or association becomes buyer to each seller of a futures contract, and seller to each buyer, and assumes responsibility for protecting buyers and sellers from financial loss by assuring performance on each contract.

Clearing House

Adjunct to commodity/stock exchanges through which transactions executed on the floor are settled. Also charged with assuring the proper conduct of delivery procedures and the adequate financing of trading.

Clearing House Funds

Payments made through a computerised clearing system. See **CHIPS** under ECONOMY, CURRENCY.

Clearing Member

Firm which is a member of a clearing house organisation. All clearing members must be exchange members, though not all exchange members need to belong to the clearing house. Non-clearing members must operate their clearing procedures through members.

Clearing Price

Daily price at which a clearing house clears all trades and settles all contracts between members for each contract month. See **Settlement Price** under COMMODITIES.

Close End of a trading session when last orders are executed.

Closed Position Opening transaction in commodities matched by a corresponding offsetting trade in the same delivery—a purchase matched by a later sale or vice versa.

Closing Out Action offsetting a long or short position. See **Square**.

Closing Price Price or price range recorded by an exchange during or at the close of a trading session. See **Settlement Price** under COMMODITIES.

Commission Pro rata remuneration for work done as an agent. Brokerage can be charged according to an official minimum scale laid down by an exchange or be subject to negotiation.

Congested Market (a) Market in which one or more individuals or groups hold concentrated positions, raising the possibility that contracts may not liquidate in an orderly fashion. (b) In technical analysis, a price range within which buying power and selling pressure are about equal, resulting in a sideways movement of prices.

Convergence The process by which cash and futures prices move toward equality as delivery approaches.

Corner To acquire control of the supply of a commodity or security so that it becomes possible to manipulate its market price. Increasingly prohibited by exchange rules and legislations.

Cover (a) Collateral deposited as security against an open position or borrowing. See **Margin**. (b) Forward contract to protect against foreign exchange fluctuations. (c) The purchase/sale of futures to offset a previously established short/long position. See entry under EQUITIES.

Day Order Order, especially in commodities, given for one day at a specific price. If it cannot be executed, it is automatically cancelled.

Day Traders Traders who acquire and liquidate the same futures position during one trading day. In the USA also known as "scalpers".

Dealer Trader in securities, currencies, commodities or financial instruments. A firm can be considered a dealer when it takes positions for its own account.

Dealer Loan Overnight loan to a dealer, backed by collateral.

Declaration Date Last date for declaring an option. See **Option** and **Expiry Date**.

Delta
The ratio by which the price of an option moves relative to the underlying futures contract or financial instrument.

Depth Of Market
Extent of business which can be done in a market without causing a price disturbance. See **Thin Market** and **Liquid Market**.

Discount
An amount paid below the normal price level. In foreign exchange terms it is a margin by which the forward rate falls below spot. Opposite to **Premium**. See entries under LENDING and COMMODITIES.

Discretionary Account
Account for which the broker or bank has a discretionary power of attorney, either completely or within set limits, from the holder to manage on his behalf.

Downside Potential
The amount of downward price movement expected by an investor or analyst. Opposite to **Upside Potential**.

Dutch Auction
Auction where the lowest price needed to sell the entire offering is the price at which all the goods being offered for sale are sold. Conducted by lowering the asking price until buyers have appeared.

Ease
Slow and/or minor decline in market prices.

Exercise Notice
When the holder of an option gives formal notice of intent to exercise his right to buy or sell the underlying stock at the previously fixed price.

Exercise Price
The price at which an option may be exercised. Also known as the strike price.

Expiry Date
Last date for exercising an option or trading a futures position. See **Declaration Date** and **Last Trading Day**.

Factor
Agent who transacts business for another on a commission basis. See **Factoring** under LENDING.

FAS
(a) In the USA, the Financial Accounting Standards which govern accounting rules. (b) In shipping, free alongside ship. A charterer's responsibility for delivering goods on quay within reach of ship's cranes etc. See **FOB** and **CIF**.

Firm
(a) Advancing market. (b) Buy or sell order which can be carried out without further confirmation during a fixed period. (c) In the foreign exchange market, a "firm" quote means a dealer is willing to trade at the rate thus quoted.

Firmer
Market which is rising, particularly after some hesitancy.

First Notice Day
The first date, varying by contracts and exchanges, on which

7

notices of intention to deliver actual financial instruments or physical commodities against futures are authorised.

Fixation
Point at which buyer or seller in a call purchase or sale on a futures market determines the price, i.e. the purchaser in a sale, the seller in a purchase. See **Call Purchase** and **Call Sale**. See **Fix** under ECONOMY, CURRENCY and **Gold Fix** under COMMODITIES.

Floor
Trading floor in a stock exchange or commodity market.

Floor Broker
Exchange member who executes orders for others on the floor of the exchange and is paid commission.

Floor Price
Minimum price which normally cannot be further reduced due to political, economic or trade considerations.

Floor Trader
Exchange member who usually effects orders on his own account, or one in which he had an interest, on the trading floor. Also referred to as a "local".

FOB
Free on Board. (a) Shipment term meaning freight and insurance costs are borne by the charterer. The transaction price includes delivery at the seller's expense to a specified point (i.e. across the rails of a ship at a particular point) before the purchaser takes responsibility for the consignment. FOB Stowed means the seller also bears all loading costs. (b) Applied to imports in balance of payments accounts to mean valuation of goods at point of embarkation. This makes imports more directly comparable to exports. See **CIF**.

Forward Market
Market in foreign exchange for future delivery or in physical commodities for later shipment. In the USA it can also mean trading outside a commodity exchange for delivery at a future date. See **Futures** under COMMODITIES.

Forward Maturities
Days beyond spot for which forward deals can be completed.

Forward Months
Months in which futures contracts for forward delivery are traded.

Fundamental Analysis
Also called fundamental research. System of analysing the basic underlying factors affecting the outlook for supply and demand for a security or commodity and the resulting price outlook. One such factor affecting commodities is weather, whereas fundamental to a company's share performance is the annual profit. See **Technical Analysis**.

Front-Running
Activity in one market based on knowledge of impending trades in another market: e.g. when a trader in the cash

equity market or in the futures market learns of an impending trade and uses the advance information to take a position in the options market.

Fungibility
Interchangeability. Something fungible can be exchanged for another answering the same description. Thus one five pound note is fungible as it can be changed for another five pound note. In a futures market, contracts for the same commodity and delivery month are fungible as such contracts have to meet standard specifications (e.g. of quality, quantity, delivery date and delivery locations). If two exchanges set the same specifications, their contracts are fungible, and a position in one can be offset by an opposing trade in the other.

Futures
See entry under COMMODITIES.

Good Till Cancelled (GTC)
Buy or sell order which remains in force until executed or cancelled by the customer. Also called Open Order.

Hardening
A slowly advancing market, or a price which is stabilising.

Hedge
Trading technique that involves taking a position in the futures market to offset a position in the cash market. Common in commodities, stock and option markets. The point of hedging is to minimise the risk of inventory loss or to lock in a profit due to price fluctuations by taking equal and opposite positions in cash and futures. See **Long Hedge, Short Hedge** and **Selling Hedge**.

Hit The Bid
Dealer's willingness in the USA to sell at the bid price or buy at the offer asked by another dealer.

In-the-Money
A call option is in-the-money if the price of the underlying instrument is higher than the exercise price. A put option is in-the-money if the price of the underlying instrument is below the exercise price. See **Out-of-the-Money**.

Inverted Market
Futures market in which the nearer months are selling at premiums to the more distant months. See **Backwardation** under COMMODITIES.

Kerb
Trading outside official market hours. On the London Metal Exchange, kerb refers to a 15 to 20 minute period at the end of each morning and afternoon session when all metals are traded simultaneously around the ring.

Last Notice Day
Final day for the issuing of notices of intent to deliver against a futures contract.

Last Trading Day
Last day for trading in the current delivery month. Futures contracts outstanding at the end of the last trading day must

be settled by delivery of underlying physical commodities or financial instruments, or by agreement for monetary settlement if the former is impossible.

Limit　　See **Price Limit**.

Life of Contract　　The period to date from the start of trading in a futures or options contract, with the maximum life of the contract being from start of trading to expiry. Life of contract highs (or lows) refer to when a contract is trading at the highest (or lowest) level so far in that contract's existence.

Limit Order　　Order in which the customer sets a limit on either price or time of execution, or both, as contrasted with a market order which implies the order be filled at the most favourable price as soon as possible. See **Market Order, Stop Order** and **Time Order**.

Liquid Market　　Market with sufficient volume for buying and selling to be accomplished with ease. See **Thin Market**.

Liquidation　　Transaction to reduce or close out a long or short position. See entry under EQUITIES.

Liquidity　　(a) Depth of a market (e.g. securities or commodities) and its ability to absorb sudden shifts in supply and demand without excessive price fluctuations. (b) Cash, or cash position, or international money supply.

Local　　See **Floor Trader**.

Locked In　　(a) Situation where an investor has made a profit on the purchase of a commodity or security, and finds his potential profit reduced if he disposes of the security or commodity, e.g. through imposition of a capital gains tax. Thus he cannot realise his gain until the investment has been held long enough to qualify for favourable tax treatment. (b) A situation when a trader cannot establish or unwind a position in a market due to a limit move. (c) Refers to a profit that is protected by a hedged position.

Long　　Buying to establish a market position but not yet closing the contract out through an offsetting sale. Opposite of **Short**.

Long Hedge　　Buying of futures contracts in expectation of actual cash market purchases. Used e.g. by processors or exporters of commodities as protection against an advance in the cash price. See **Hedge**.

Long Interest　　Long holdings or contracts in any given futures markets.

Long The Basis　　Person or firm buying a spot commodity and hedging with a sale of futures is "long the basis". Basis is the price differential between spot and futures at a given location. See **Basis** under COMMODITIES.

Maintenance Margin
Margin, normally less than, but still part of, the original margin which must be maintained on deposit at all times.

Margin
(a) Incremental percentage referring to deposits, collateral or permissible exchange rate fluctuations. See entries under EQUITIES and COMMODITIES. (b) In futures, it refers to cash deposited with the broker for each contract as a guarantee of fulfilment of the contract. Also called a security deposit. See **Margin Call** under COMMODITIES.

Market Amount
Amount normally considered the minimum for dealings in a market, especially foreign exchange.

Market Forces
Conditions of supply and demand which operate in a free market to determine prices through the decisions of buyers and sellers, lenders and borrowers.

Market Maker
Recognised financial institution or individual making consistent buy and sell quotations in a selection of issues in the secondary market. A principal requisite is that the market maker must hold or have ready access to the issues quoted, i.e. carry an inventory. See entry under EQUITIES.

Market Order
Order to buy and sell a security or a futures contract at the best price obtainable at the time it is entered in the market. See **Limit Order**, **Stop Order** and **Time Order**.

Market Participant
One who buys and sells on behalf of clients and on his own account.

Market Trend
General direction, ignoring short term fluctuations, of price movements in a market.

Market Value
Current trading price, the level at which something can be bought and sold. Also the value of fixed assets, e.g. plant and equipment.

Match
Two offsetting transactions either on a dealer's own account or for one or more customers.

Matched Book
A situation where the maturity dates for a bank's or trader's liabilities match those of his assets. It can also mean that borrowing costs equal the interest earned on loans.

Maximum/ Minimum Price Fluctuation
Maximum or minimum movement allowed in the price of a futures contract in all or part of a trading session.

Members Rate	Commission charged for executing an order on behalf of an exchange member.
Metre	3.28084275 ft. A cubic metre equals 35.3148 cu. ft.
Naked Position	Unhedged long or short position. See **Hedge**.
Net Change	Difference between the closing price on one day and the closing price on the following day in which the stock, currency or commodity is traded.
Net Position	Difference between the open long contracts and open short contracts held by a trader in various delivery months of any one commodity on a futures market.
Nominal Price	Estimated price quoted in the absence of actual transaction, normally an average between the last bid and the last offer.
Offer	Willing to sell at a given price. Opposite to **Bid**. See **Asked Price**.
Offered Market	When offers outnumber bids in a given market. Opposite to **Bid Market**.
Offered Rate	Rate at which a bank or dealer is prepared to do business.
Open Contracts	Contracts which have been bought or sold without the transaction having been completed by subsequent sale or purchase, or making or taking actual delivery of the financial instrument or physical commodity.
Open Interest	Number of open futures contracts. Refers to unliquidated purchases or sales. See **Open Position** under COMMODITIES.
Open Order	See **Good Till Cancelled**.
Open Outcry	Method of public trading required in some commodity, options and stock markets for making bids and offers. Dealers literally "cry out" or shout their proposed transactions.
Opening Price	Price recorded during a period designated by an exchange as the beginning of trading.
Option	Right, acquired for a price, to buy certain specified property, e.g. a security or an instrument (call option), or to sell it at an agreed price (put option), within a specified time. See **Call Option, Put Option, At-The-Money, In-The-Money, Out-Of-The-Money, Exercise Notice, Expiry Date** and **Writer**.
Out-Of-The-Money	A call option is out-of-the-money if the price of the underlying instrument is lower than the exercise price. A put

option is out-of-the-money if the instrument's price is above the exercise price. See **In-The-Money**.

Overbought   Situation where rates or prices of a currency, commodity or security may have advanced too far in response to net buying pressure, thus creating a vulnerable market.

Overnight   Deal from the current trading day to the next. At weekends, this means Friday to Monday.

Oversold   Situation where prices have declined too steeply and too rapidly in relation to a market's underlying fundamental factors. The likelihood is that the market will then start to rise.

Point   Used in describing changes in stock/bond prices or exchange and interest rates, e.g. in the US stock market one point equals one dollar, while for bonds with a 1,000 dollar face value it is equal to 10 dollars. See **Basis Point**.

Position   (a) Client's status on the securities or commodities market as represented by unliquidated long or short open contracts. (b) A commodity in a convenient location for delivery or shipment is termed "in position".

Premium   (a) A margin paid above the normal price level. It may reflect market conditions. Near delivery and higher quality can put one futures contract at a premium over another. (b) The amount by which a bond sells above par. (c) In foreign exchange terms it is the margin by which the forward exchange rate is higher than the spot. Opposite to **Discount**.

Price-Fix Buying/Selling   Method whereby an outright price is established for a physical commodity by the unwinding of a futures hedge on a physicals position.

Price Limit   Maximum permitted advance or decline in a market during a trading session. Also the specified price in a limit order. In the futures market limits are set by the exchanges and can be altered depending on market volatility.

Profit-Taking   Covering a long or short position in a market to realise gains. Mostly, however, the term refers to selling, e.g. disposing of shares at a higher price than that at which they were bought.

Put Option   Option to sell stocks, commodities or financial instruments at an agreed price within a specified time, made in expectation of falling prices. In the Eurobond market a put option means the investor has the right to sell the bond back to the borrower before the final maturity at a fixed price.

Quotation Current price or rate of a commodity, security or currency on the market place, or exchange, but not necessarily the price at which a trade will be made.

Rally Rise or recovery in prices after a decline.

Range High and low prices, or high and low bids and offers recorded during a specified time.

Reaction When prices decline after gaining, or rise after falling.

Realise Sell an asset.

Recovery See **Rally**.

Resistance Barrier Price level above or below which a market may find difficulty in moving, partly the reflection of chartist sentiment. Mostly used, however, when the market is moving higher. See **Support Point**.

Resting Order Order to purchase at a price lower than, or sell at a higher price than the prevailing market level.

Retendering The right of holders of certain futures contracts who have been tendered a delivery notice via the clearing house to redeliver against the same futures position.

Risk Aversion Degree to which an investor is unwilling to assume a risk.

Risk Premium Return or extra reward for assuming risks.

Scale Down To buy at regular price intervals in a declining market. Scale up is to sell at similar regular price intervals in a rising market.

Scalp To trade for small gains, normally by establishing and liquidating a position within the same day. Larger gains can be made by taking many positions during a trading session. See **Day Traders**.

Seller's Market Market in which sellers hold the advantage because buyers are prepared to buy, at existing prices, larger amounts than sellers are currently able to produce or prepared to market. See **Buyer's Market**.

Seller's Option Option for a seller to decide, provided the standard contract terms are observed, the time and place of delivery and/or the quality of commodity or security supplied in execution of an order.

Selling Hedge Also known as a short hedge. Involves selling a futures contract as protection against a future fall in price of the actual financial instrument or physical commodity. See **Hedge**.

Settlement Date   Date on which payment for a transaction must be made. See **Trade Date**.

Settlement Price   See entry under COMMODITIES.

Short   A sale of e.g. a futures or options contract but not yet closing it out through an offsetting purchase. Opposite to **Long**.

Short Covering   Buying to offset a short position. See **Bear Covering**.

Short Hedge   See **Selling Hedge**.

Short Interest   (a) Number of stocks needed to be purchased to cover short sales. See **Short Sale**. (b) Short holdings or contracts in a futures market.

Short Sale   Sale of stocks, bonds, foreign exchange or commodities that the seller does not own, made in anticipation of a fall in prices.

Soft Market   When supply surpasses demand and pronounced price falls occur on minimal selling pressure.

Speculator   A recognised participant in most markets, who tries to anticipate price changes, and, e.g. through buying and selling futures contracts, aims to make profits. Generally the speculator has no involvement in the underlying physical commodity or financial instrument.

Spot   Price at which a currency or physical commodity is selling for immediate or very near delivery, i.e. two days in the case of foreign exchange. It is the cash sale price as opposed to a futures price. See **Cash Market** under COMMODITIES and **Spot Market** under ENERGY.

Spread   See entries under LENDING and COMMODITIES.

Square   When purchases and sales are in balance, i.e. when a position is neither short nor long.

Stop Order (Stop Loss Order)   Order to a stock or commodity broker to buy or sell at the market when a given price threshold is reached. See **Limit Order**, **Market Order** and **At Best**.

Straddle   (a) In commodities, the simultaneous matching purchase of one delivery with the sale of another. See **Spread**. (b) In stock markets, a contract giving the holder the right to buy or sell at a certain price. (c) In options trading, a simultaneously held "put and call" giving the holder the right to buy and sell at a certain price.

Strike Price   See **Exercise Price**.

Strong Market   When there are more buyers than sellers and the overall price trend is upward.

Support Point   (a) Point at which a central bank may intervene in a currency, usually its own. (b) Level at which market forces and/or charts may combine to prevent further price declines for a currency, security or commodity etc. See **Resistance Barrier**.

Swap   Generally, the exchange of one entitlement for another, or the exchange of streams of payments between two counterparties. See **Currency Swap** under ECONOMY, CURRENCY and **Interest Rate Swap** under LENDING.

Switching   (a) In commodities, the transfer of an open position into another delivery through the simultaneous liquidation of one futures commitment and the establishment of another in the same market. (b) In securities, selling stocks or bonds and replacing them with others in the hope of improving profit prospects.

Tap   To seek financing through the issue of shares, stock or bonds on stock or capital markets. See **Tap Stock** under LENDING.

Technical Analysis   Analysis of securities and commodities markets through the use of pertinent technical data regarding price changes and changes in trading volume etc. See **Charting** and **Fundamental Analysis**.

Technical Decline/Rally   Movement in market prices reflecting the impact of technical internal market factors such as volume, delivery conditions or chartist influence, as opposed to outside supply/demand factors.

Tender   (a) Notice of intent to deliver physical goods against a commodity futures contract. See **Tender** under COMMODITIES. (b) An invitation to suppliers to offer plant or goods to meet requirements. (c) A means of offering bonds or treasury bills to the market. See **Tender Offer** under EQUITIES.

Thin Market   Market as a whole, or for a single commodity or security etc. in which there is little buying or selling interest, little volume or activity.

Tick   Minimum possible price movement up or down in a contract.

Tight Market
Active and competitive market combining considerable volume with narrow spreads between bid and asked prices.

Time (Limit) Order
Order to buy or sell on a market at a specific time. It may occur at a stated time of day, at the opening, close or mid-session or some time during a week. See **Limit Order, Market Order** and **Stop Order**.

Trade Date
Day on which a deal is carried out or completed. The settlement date may be the same or later.

Trade House
Trading concern acting on behalf of customers as well as on its own account.

Tradeable Amount
Minimum quantity accepted for trading in a market. See **Unit of Trading**.

Trading Limit
(a) Maximum amount of a commodity which can be bought or sold by an individual in a single day. (b) Maximum futures position permitted to be held by any individual. (c) Maximum permitted price movements in any single day.

Trustee
(a) Institution in which the rights of the bond or note holders may be vested. (b) A person holding title to a property for the benefit of another person.

Two Way Market
Market where dealers actively quote both buying and selling rates.

Unit of Trading
Minimum quantity in which trading can take place in, for example, a commodity or security.

Unload
Market term for dumping a substantial amount of a commodity, currency, security or other goods on a market at a low price with intent to (a) simply dispose of the asset being sold at any cost, (b) make a profit by low price volume sales, thus undercutting other market suppliers.

Unwinding
Disengagement of a financial, leads-and-lags, or a spread speculative position. See **Leads and Lags** under ECONOMY, CURRENCY.

Upside Potential
The amount of upward price movement expected by an investor or analyst. Opposite to "**downside potential**".

Value Date
In the Eurocurrency and foreign exchange markets refers to the delivery date of funds to settle the transaction. In the Eurobond market the value date falls seven calendar days after the deal is struck, regardless of holidays.

Value Spot
Spot deal for settlement in two trading days.

Variable Margin Call

Call made in a clearing house to a clearing member during trading, when price movements have substantially reduced the clearing member's margin deposits. It is payable within the hour. See **Margin**.

Volatile Market

Sensitive market changing direction rapidly and erratically.

Volume

Total number of transactions made during a specified period.

Warrant

See entries under LENDING and COMMODITIES.

Weak Market

When there are more sellers than buyers, and the general price trend is down. Opposite to **Strong Market**.

Whipsawed

Term describing a dealer caught in a volatile market with losing positions.

Wire House

In the USA, a member of an exchange with an internal communications network.

Writer

Seller of an option contract. See **Option**.

Economy, Currency

Above The Line That part of a government budget concerned with revenue, mainly taxes and expenditure. A treasury or finance ministry normally budgets for a surplus above the line for demand management purposes. For corporations it means all income and expenses before tax. See **Below the Line**.

Across The Board Tariff Negotiations Negotiations involving uniform percentage reductions or increase in duties on major categories of items. The opposite is item by item tariff negotiation.

Adjustable Peg Exchange rate regime in which a currency is "pegged" or "fixed" in relation to another currency, frequently the US dollar, with the rate being adjusted from time to time.

Adjustment Change in the official currency rate or in internal economic policies to correct a payments imbalance.

Adjustment Process International system and operation of payments adjustment policies e.g. exchange rate alignment, changes in government expenditure, exchange controls.

Adjustment Trigger Objective criterion impelling exchange rate or economic policy adjustment.

Ad Valorem Tax or duty levied as a fixed percentage of an item's value as opposed to a fixed unitary levy e.g. stamp duties. Latin term meaning "according to value".

AFESD Arab Fund for Economic and Social Development, based in Kuwait and established in 1968.

African Development Bank (ADB) Based in Abidjan and founded in 1964.

Aggregate Demand Total demand for goods and services in the economy. It comprises household demand for consumer goods and services; demand from firms and government for investment goods; demand by local and central government for goods and services; demands of consumers and firms in other countries for goods and services, i.e. exports.

Aggregate Risk Total exposure of a bank to any single customer for both spot and forward contracts.

Aggregate Supply Total supply of goods and services in the economy available to meet aggregate demand. This is made up of domestically produced goods and imports.

Agio

Difference in value between currencies. Also used as a term to describe the percentage charged on changing paper money into cash, or a weak currency into a strong currency.

ALADI

Asociación Latino-Americana de Integración or Latin American Integration Association. Based in Montevideo with 11 members, its purpose is to establish reciprocal trade arrangements in the region.

Amstel Club

Grouping of finance houses from 15 European countries which make reciprocal arrangements to finance trade, especially for the smaller exporter. The official title is Amstel Finance International AG.

Andean Pact

Based in Lima, this group of five South American nations aims to establish a free trade area, and complement their industries. Members are Venezuela, Colombia, Ecuador, Peru and Bolivia. The five countries in 1978 set up an Andean Reserve Fund, based in Bogota, to help them with balance of payment problems. They decided in 1988 to open it up to other countries of the continent and transform it into a Latin American Reserve Fund.

Appreciation

Increase in market value of currency's exchange rate, a capital asset or financial paper.

Arab Bank for Economic Development in Africa (ABEDA)

Established in 1973 and based in Khartoum, this international institution channels Arab capital into non-Arab Africa for development projects.

Arab Monetary Fund

Based in Abu Dhabi and formed in 1977 by the Council for Arab Economic Unity. Members are Saudi Arabia, Algeria, Bahrain, Egypt, Iraq, Jordan, Kuwait, Lebanon, Libya, Mauritania, Morocco, Oman, Qatar, Somalia, Sudan, Syria, United Arab Emirates, Tunisia, Yemen Arab Republic, People's Democratic Republic of Yemen and the Palestine Liberation Organisation. The fund's unit of account is the Arab accounting dinar.

Arbitration

Settlement of a difference usually arising from a contract by referring the dispute to one or more independent persons rather than instituting legal proceedings. Arbitration must be agreed and cannot be imposed. It tends to be simpler, quicker, and cheaper than legal proceedings.

Around

Foreign exchange market term to quote forward premiums or discounts with the par point understood. E.g. ten-ten around means 10 points on either side of par, i.e. the current spot rate.

Article Eight Currency	A "senior currency" according to the IMF definition. It should be convertible and free from controls.
ASEAN	Association of South East Asian Nations formed in 1967 with its headquarters in Jakarta. Members are Brunei, Malaysia, Indonesia, Singapore, Philippines and Thailand.
Asian Clearing Union	Joint arrangement for settling international payments imbalances between Bangladesh, Burma, India, Iran, Nepal, Pakistan and Sri Lanka. However, payments for trade between India and Nepal are settled outside the union. The Asian Monetary Unit is used as the unit of account.
Asian Currency Unit (ACU)	Separate accounting unit used in Singapore by selected banks licensed to deal in non-resident deposits.
Asian Development Bank (ADB)	Founded in 1966 and based in Manila.
Asian Monetary Unit	Accounting unit for the Asian Clearing Union with a value equal to the Special Drawing Rights (SDRs) issued by the International Monetary Fund.
Association Cambiste Internationale	Paris-based International Association of Foreign Exchange dealers.
Authorised Dealer	Bank, financial institution authorised by government agency or central bank to deal in foreign exchange. It can also cover authorisation to deal in securities or commodities for traders in these sectors.
Balance For Official Financing	Used in the UK balance of payments statistics, and comprises current account balance, total investment and other capital flows plus a balancing item covering errors and omissions. It is equal to the changes in the reserves together with total official borrowing or lending.
Balance Of Payments (BOP)	Systematic record of one country's net transactions with the rest of the world over a given period. It includes trade, services, capital movements and unilateral transfers. Current account balance of payments comprises imports and exports of merchandise, as well as payments and receipts for services such as shipping, banking and tourism. It also involves private transfers (e.g. remittances from migrant workers) and official transfers (e.g. contributions to international bodies such as the EC). The capital account comprises: (a) long-term flows, such as those used for investment in land and plant, and (b) short-term flows, such as those chasing profits from appreciating currencies or high interest rates on deposits.

Basic balance is a term often used to refer to current account plus long-term capital account. By adding short-term capital to basic balance, we arrive at what many countries call their overall balance of payments.

Balance of Trade Monetary record of a country's net imports and exports of physical merchandise.

Balanced Budget Budgetary situation where expenditure matches revenue. Also called a neutral budget.

Band Maximum permitted range within which a currency is allowed to move against a reference currency. See **European Monetary System**.

Bank for International Settlements (BIS) Profit-making clearing agency based in Basle for central bank shareholder members in foreign exchange and Eurocurrency markets. The US Federal Reserve Board is not a member for technical reasons, and the US shareholding is through Citibank. The BIS acts as a principal forum for routine meetings of central bank governors, which a senior US Fed official attends. Its financial accounts are denominated in Swiss gold francs. Dividends are paid annually in dollars at the day's Zurich Swiss franc spot rate.

Bank Return Weekly or monthly statement issued by a central bank showing its financial position in summary form.

Barter Exchange of goods or services for other goods or services. No money is exchanged. See **Compensation Trade, Counter-Trade**.

Base Currency Currency against which exchange rates are normally quoted in a given centre or country, e.g. the US dollar or sterling.

Base Year Year chosen as the base for an economic index.

Basic Balance Balance of payments on current and long term capital account. See **Balance of Payments**.

Below The Line That part of a budget concerning receipts relating to the redemption of debt and expenditure to be financed by borrowing. See **Above The Line**.

Benchmark Actual measurement of economic data in a specific time period, used as a basis for comparison.

Berne Union Established in 1934 to study export credit insurance techniques. The full title is the International Union of Credit and Investment Insurers.

Bilateral Clearing Often used in international trade between developing countries and East Bloc states. Trade and other payments are balanced and settled once yearly by the central banks involved. Settlements often take place in convertible currencies.

BIS
See **Bank for International Settlements**.

Black Economy
That portion of a nation's output of goods and services which (illegally) escapes taxation.

Black Market
Buying and selling of prohibited or controlled goods or currencies through illegal dealers.

Blocked Currency
Currency whose use is controlled by the government of issue. Such currency can only be used for purchases within the country.

Book
Term used by foreign exchange dealers, for example, to mean their total exposure to the market. The reduction of this exposure to zero is known as book-squaring.

Boom
Rapid and sustained rise in prices and general business activity.

Border Tax Adjustment
Under GATT rules, border tax adjustments are permitted on internationally traded goods. Exports may be relieved of indirect taxes and imports taxed an amount equivalent to indirect taxes on similar domestic goods. No adjustment is allowed for direct taxes.

Bretton Woods
Site in New Hampshire, USA, where in 1944 an international conference was held to work out rules for a post-war international monetary system. It resulted in the creation of the International Monetary Fund and the World Bank. The system was based on fixed exchange rates combined with temporary financing facilities to overcome crises. Devaluation was only allowed in the case of a fundamental disequilibrium in a country's balance of payments. When, following consistently large American payments deficits, the dollar in 1971 ceased to be convertible into gold at the then official 35 dollars per ounce price, the Bretton Woods system was brought down, heralding an era of floating currencies.

Broken Period
Forward foreign exchange deal for a non-standard period. Standard periods are, for example, one, two, three, six and twelve months.

Budget
Official or governmental statement of actual or projected revenue and expenditure. Can also apply to corporate financial planning.

Bundesbank
The West German central bank, based in Frankfurt. Its credit

policies are set by its Central Bank Council, which normally meets every second Thursday and consists of board (directorate) members and the heads of its regional arms (Landeszentralbank) which run its operations in Germany's 11 Federal States. See **Money Stock**.

Business Cycle

Alternative expansion and contraction or acceleration and deceleration in overall business activity shown by fluctuations in the economic aggregates.

Cable

Foreign exchange market term for the dollar/sterling spot exchange rate.

Cable Transfer

Transfer of money by cable between two centres.

Cairns Group

See entry under COMMODITIES.

Cambiste

Foreign exchange dealer.

Capital Account

(a) Balance of payment items not included in the current account, including investment and deposit funds, aid and military expenditure. See **Balance Of Payments**. (b) Also used in US accounting to indicate the amount of equity in a business.

Capital Exports

See entry under LENDING.

Capital Formation

Net addition to capital stock in a given period.

CARICOM

Based in Georgetown, Guyana. The 13-member Caribbean Community and Common Market was founded to establish a regional free trade area.

Central Bank

Major regulatory bank in a nation's monetary system, generally government controlled. Its role normally includes control of the credit system, the note issue, supervision of commercial banks, management of exchange reserves and the national currency's value as well as acting as the government's banker.

Central Bank Intervention

To influence monetary conditions, a central bank can intervene by imposing direct controls on interest rates, foreign exchange etc, or by acting in the open market (i.e. through buying and selling currencies or bonds etc.). When intervening in currency markets, the bank may simply be seeking to stabilise them rather than to steer exchange rates to any particular level.

Central Rate

Exchange rate against the European Currency Unit (ECU) adopted for each currency within the European Monetary System (EMS). Central rates are used to tie together member currencies of the EMS exchange rate mechanism (ERM), linking them in a parity grid which allows for fluctuations within strict limits. See **European Currency Unit** and **European Monetary System**.

Certificate Of Origin
Establishes the country of origin for imported goods. It enables the customs authorities to determine whether the goods can benefit from preferential tariff rates due to their country of origin. Issued by Chambers of Commerce and similar bodies.

CFA Franc
Communauté Financière Africaine franc used mainly in former French Central and West African colonies. It has a fixed parity against the French franc. See **Franc Zone**.

CFP Franc
French Pacific Community franc used in departments and overseas territories in the Pacific.

Chicago School
Free market philosophy school of monetarists, centred on the University of Chicago and associated with Professor Milton Friedman.

CHIPS
Clearing House Interbank Payment System. A computerised clearing system in New York bringing together members of the New York Clearing House and others.

Clean Float
Flotation of a currency on foreign exchange markets without official intervention. Opposite to **Dirty Float**.

Closed Economy
In theory an economy completely closed to international trade with no exports, imports or capital movements. In practice where trade and capital movements are severely restricted.

CMEA
See **COMECON**.

COCOM
Established in 1949, the Paris-based Coordinating Committee for Multilateral Export Controls (COCOM) groups NATO countries (except Iceland) and Japan. It compiles lists of goods considered to be of strategic importance and therefore not to be sold by the West to East bloc countries.

Coincident Indicator
Measure of economic activity that moves broadly in line with the general business cycle, such as industrial production and retail sales.

COMECON
The Council for Mutual Economic Assistance (CMEA or COMECON) established in 1949 with headquarters in Moscow to coordinate the economic development of member countries. It now comprises Bulgaria, Cuba, Czechoslovakia, German Democratic Republic, Hungary, Mongolia, Poland, Romania, Vietnam and the USSR. Albania is a non-active member.

Common Market
See **European Communities**.

Compensation Trade
System under which an exporter accepts that part of the purchase price is paid for by goods from the importing country. See **Barter, Counter-Trade**.

Competitive Devaluation
Devaluation designed to gain a competitive advantage in export markets.

Composite Index
Average or combined index of dissimilar component series. The US Department of Commerce has a closely followed composite index of 12 leading economic indicators.

Comptroller Of The Currency
US Treasury Department official responsible for chartering national banks and with primary supervisory authority over them. All national banks must be members of the Federal Reserve system, and are insured by the Federal Deposit Insurance Corporation.

Consolidated Fund
Funds in the UK standing to the account of the Exchequer into which revenue is paid from taxation and which is used to finance government expenditure.

Consumer Price Index (CPI)
Monthly index measuring the change in the cost of a basket of consumer essentials—food, rent, mortgages, clothing, heating, fuel, travel etc. A major indicator of a nation's inflation rate. See **Retail Price Index**.

Consumer Spending
Expenditure on goods and services for immediate consumption by households and an indicator of the level of economic activity.

Convertibility
Monetary term loosely used to describe exchangeability of a currency into gold or SDRs. More properly, it refers to the free and uncontrolled exchangeability of one currency into another.

Coreper
Committees of Permanent Representatives to the European Community, grouping member states' ambassadors and experts, which meet at least once a week to review EC policy and negotiate decisions before they come up for approval by the Council of Ministers. See **European Communities**.

Corset
A limitation on the growth in bank lending in the UK Abandoned in 1980.

Cost Of Living Index
Roughly equivalent to, though often broader than, **Consumer** or **Retail Price Index**.

Cost-Push Inflation
When excessive wage rises push up manufacturing costs resulting in higher prices, which in turn stimulate further wage rises. Opposite to **demand-pull**.

Counter-Trade	Includes (a) Barter, the exchange of goods or services, where no money is paid over. (b) Counter-purchase, an agreement by a seller to spend all or part of his receipts on purchases from the buyer. (c) Buy-back, a deal under which a company opens a plant abroad and agrees to buy all or part of its output.
Countervailing Duty	Import duty imposed over and above normal levels when an importing country considers the export price to contain a subsidy.
Covered Interest Arbitrage	Borrowing a currency followed by conversion into a second currency for investment, then selling the second currency for future delivery against the first currency.
Crawling Peg	Technique to allow exchange rates slowly but steadily to appreciate/depreciate, either automatically or with deliberate guidance.
Cross Rate	The exchange rate between two currencies, neither of which is the US dollar. The rate is either a derivative of the exchange rates of each currency against the dollar, or a direct rate set by a bank between two non-dollar currencies.
Currency Availability	Agreement allowing lending to take place in a currency other than that intended due to its non-availability.
Currency Band	Margin within which a currency is permitted to move. See **Band**.
Currency Basket	Cocktail of currencies individually weighted and whose combined value is the equivalent of one unit. See **European Currency Unit (ECU)**.
Currency Clause	Used in contracts to set a fixed rate between two currencies, to avoid the impact of devaluation or revaluation.
Currency Swap	(a) Purchase (or sale) of a spot currency and a simultaneous sale (or purchase) in the forward market. (b) An agreement between two parties to exchange future payments in one currency for payments in a second currency. See **Swap** under GENERAL MARKET TERMS, and **Interest Rate Swap** under LENDING.
Current Account	Balance of payments embracing a country's physical imports/exports and international transactions in invisible goods and services, such as shipping, tourism and banking. See **Balance Of Payments**.
Customs Duty	Border tax usually levied on imports.
Customs Union	Agreement by a group of countries to abolish internal tariffs and adopt a uniform or common external tariff.

Dear Money   When the cost of funds produces a constricted borrowing environment.

Deficit   Shortfall (a) in balance of trade measuring net imports. (b) In balance of payments measures net foreign payments and incurred liabilities. (c) In a budget measures outlays net of revenues.

Deficit Financing   See entry under LENDING.

Deflation   Decline in prices associated with a contraction in the supply of money and credit and accompanied by a decline in output and rise in unemployment. See **Disinflation**.

Deflator   Difference between real and nominal Gross National Product, measuring the overall inflation rate in the economy. See **Gross National Product**.

Demand-Pull   Also called demand-led inflation, classically defined as too much money chasing too few goods. Opposite to **Cost-Push**.

Depression   Prolonged period of low economic activity. See **Recession**.

Devaluation   Formal downward adjustment of a currency's official par value or central exchange rate. Opposite to **Revaluation**.

Development Assistance Committee (DAC)   OECD committee charged with promoting financial assistance for developing countries.

Differential Tariff   Tariff which gives preference to, or discriminates against, certain goods from a country or group of countries, or a mixture of both.

Direct Quotation   Foreign exchange quotation which expresses a foreign currency in terms of the domestic currency.

Dirty Float   Floating currency when controlled by intervention of the authorities, i.e. not moving freely according to market conditions. Opposite to **Clean Float**.

Discount   See entries under GENERAL MARKET TERMS and LENDING.

Disequilibrium   Imbalance of national or world payments. Under the Bretton Woods system countries were theoretically obliged to adjust their exchange rate or economies when their payments balances moved into fundamental disequilibrium.

Disinflation   Slowing down of the rate at which prices rise, either via deliberate government efforts or natural causes such as economic depression. See **Deflation**.

Disposable Income

Earnings after tax or take home income. Broader than discretionary income, which is net of fixed personal spending commitments as well as tax.

Dumping

Selling goods in a market at low cost, or possibly below cost. It normally involves large quantities of goods sold to export markets. In the USA, selling stock heavily with little concern for the effect of this on the price or the market.

Easy Money

Lavish availability of credit and money associated with a relaxed monetary policy. Normally, but not always, accompanied by moderate or low interest rates.

EC

See **European Communities**.

ECLA

UN Latin American Economic Commission. Based in Santiago, it prepares studies on the region's economy.

Econometrics

Use of statistical and mathematical methods to verify and develop economic theories. It also covers the development of plans and implementation of policies based on economic findings.

Economic And Social Committee

Advisory body appointed by the EC Council of Ministers representing employers, employees and other interest groups. However it has lost much of its influence since Members of the European Parliament were directly elected from 1979.

Economic Indicators

Key statistics showing an economy's direction e.g. trade, inflation and unemployment.

Effective Exchange Rate

Composite rate, normally presented as an index intended to reflect the overall performance of a currency against its main trading partners, on a trade weighted basis.

EFTA

European Free Trade Association which groups Austria, Iceland, Norway, Finland, Sweden and Switzerland. Its general aim it to promote liberal trade practices in Europe; in particular, it seeks closer ties with the European Community.

EFTPOS

Electronic Funds Transfer at Point-of-Sale. One example is the use of plastic cards to debit a shopping bill to a bank account through a computer terminal at a retail store.

EFTS

Electronic Funds Transfer System whih switches funds electronically, thus avoiding the use of paper, e.g. automatic teller machines in banking.

Elasticity

Relative response of one variable to a small percentage change in another, e.g. the degree of change in demand for manufactured exports in response to an exchange rate adjustment. The level of demand for necessities (i.e. food) is said to be inelastic because such purchases cannot be postponed. Demand for luxuries may slow after a price increase, which is described as elastic. Supply is said to be elastic if a rise in price means a rise in production.

Eligible Liabilities

Liabilities included in establishing UK banks' reserve asset ratios.

Embargo

Prohibition (often official) on the movement by land, sea or air of certain goods, or a ban on trade in general between two countries or a group of countries.

EMS

See **European Monetary System**.

Entrepôt

Literally a warehouse. Also a major international trading centre to which goods are shipped for re-export elsewhere, i.e. entrepôt trade.

Equilibrium

Balance or near balance in a country's external payments position, or in the payments balances of a group of major IMF nations.

Escalator Clause

(a) Clause in a wage contract giving automatic pay increases when the cost of living rises beyond agreed thresholds.
(b) Clause in a contract, typically a capital project, allowing a price increase payable to the contractor to help offset cost inflation.

Escrow

Agreement or deed involving three parties. The third party is responsible for the custody of the deed, which does not take legal effect until the grantee (the person obtaining a benefit from the performance of the deed) fulfils certain conditions.

European Currency Unit (ECU)

A notional EC currency based on a basket of 10 member currencies, i.e. all except Spain and Portugal which are due to participate in the ECU from 1989. Each currency's share in the basket is weighted according to each state's share of EC output. The ECU is at the centre of the EMS and is being increasingly used in its own right for trading purposes and to denominate bond issues.

European Communities (EC)

A group of 12 West European nations normally referred to in the singular as the European Community. It amalgamates the European Coal and Steel Community (set up in 1952) with the European Economic Community and the European Atomic Energy Community (both set up in 1957).
Original members Belgium, France, Italy, Luxembourg, Netherlands and West Germany were joined in 1973 by Britain, Denmark and Ireland, in 1981 by Greece and in 1986 by Spain and Portugal.

A 17-member EC executive commission has the sole right to propose EC policies but cannot decide them. Decisions are a prerogative of the 12 member governments meeting as the EC Council of Ministers. However, the commission enjoys discretionary powers for implementing the EC's policies and is the guardian of EC treaties. See **European Parliament**.

European Free Trade Association

See **EFTA**.

European Investment Bank (EIB)

Long term financing body of the EC, which also provides soft loans to developing countries associated with the community.

European Monetary Cooperation Fund

Also known by the French abbreviation FECOM. Finances and settles claims by EC central banks on each other resulting from intervention under the European Monetary System.

European Monetary System

Formally introduced in 1979 and expanded to include all EC currencies, except the Spanish peseta and Portuguese escudo, which are due to join from 1989. Member currencies determine the value of the EC's composite currency, the European Currency Unit (ECU). Of the 10 current members all, except Britain and Greece, participate in the system's Exchange Rate Mechanism (ERM). This limits to 2.25 per cent the maximum fluctuation of member currencies against each other (although Italy is an exception and its lira can move by up to six per cent). From time to time, when participating countries recognise that defending this limitation imposes too great a strain, the central rates of ERM currencies are realigned. See **European Currency Unit**.

European Parliament

Directly elected assembly for representatives of EC member states. On most issue its role is purely consultative. The major exception is the budget where it shares decision-making powers with the Council of Ministers (which represents EC governments). It is also the only body which can dismiss the EC's executive commission. See **European Communities**.

Eurostat

The EC's statistics office, based in Luxembourg.

Excess Liquidity

Banks having liquidity, cash or cash instruments, over and above their normal requirements.

Excess Reserves

US bank-held reserves with the Federal Reserve in excess of requirements. It is the difference between total reserves elgible to meet reserve requirements and required reserves that must be held.

Exchange Controls

Regulations designed to restrict or prevent certain foreign currency transactions mainly by a country's nationals. Also likely to cover movement of precious metals, especially gold and silver. Controls are used to maintain and protect a country's financial position and the value of its currency.

Exchange Equalisation Account

Account controlled by the UK Treasury and managed by the Bank of England. Its assets include the country's gold and foreign exchange reserves and the objective is to manage the exchange in line with government policy. Many countries operate similar accounts. In the USA and France they are known as Exchange Stabilisation Funds.

Exchange Rate

Rate at which a currency is exchanged for another currency, gold or Special Drawing Rights. See **Parity**.

Exchange Rate Mechanism (ERM)

See **European Monetary System**.

Exotic Currencies

Currencies which are infrequently dealt, and in which there is no international market of any size.

Export Houses

Trading houses specialising in selling virtually all categories of goods throughout the world. They can handle all aspects of international trade, including finance.

Export Quota

Bilateral or multilateral agreement between countries governing exports of industrial or other goods. See entry under COMMODITIES.

Exposure

On foreign exchange markets, exposure can arise through the existence of an uncovered position, whether overall or for a single currency. The extent of exposure can reflect the different maturity periods for the currencies being used. See entry under LENDING.

External Accounts

Accounts in a national currency maintained for use by non-residents.

FECOM

See **European Monetary Cooperation Fund**.

Federal Reserve System

Known as the Fed, this is the central banking system of the United States comprising 12 Federal Reserve Banks controlling 12 districts under the Federal Reserve Board in Washington. Membership of the Fed is obligatory for banks chartered by the US Comptroller of Currency and voluntary for banks chartered with state charters. All member banks subscribe to its capital and around 70 per cent of US bank deposits are held by member banks. The 12 Fed banks are based in Boston, New York, Philadelphia, Cleveland, Richmond, Atlanta, Chicago, St Louis, Dallas, Minneapolis,

Kansas City and San Francisco. See **Federal Open Market Committee** under LENDING.

FELABAN
The Bogota-based Latin American Banking Federation, which groups the banking associations of Latin American countries.

Fine Tuning
Flexible fiscal and monetary policy action designed to achieve precise short term patterns of economic performance.

First Line Reserves
Currency component of a central bank's monetary reserves, a non-US term.

Fiscal Drag
Inhibiting effect on private economic activity of the automatic growth in government revenue taken from its income and cash resources. The drag refers to the weight of higher taxes on higher incomes so that after-tax incomes do not reflect the extent of a wage rise.

Fiscal Policy
The means by which a government influences the economy through its budget by changes in tax and welfare payments and/or government spending. See **Monetary Policy**.

Fiscal Year
See **Financial Year** under EQUITIES.

Fix
On some foreign exchange markets or bourses a daily meeting (fixing) at which the rates for different currencies are officially fixed by adjusting the buying and selling level to reflect market conditions. Participants include commercial banks and directly or indirectly the central bank. The latter may intervene to maintain the rate at a specific level. See **Gold Fix** under COMMODITIES.

Fixed Exchange Rate
Exchange value with fixed parities, or central rate relationships with SDRs, gold, the US dollar or other currencies. See **Special Drawing Rights (SDRs)**.

Flexible Tariff
In the USA a tariff designed to even out differences between the cost of imported and domestically produced goods.

Float
(a) Condition under which a currency is allowed to fluctuate outside internationally prescribed limits without discretionary intervention, i.e. free float. See **Dirty Float**.
(b) To launch an issue, company or business. (c) In the USA, term to describe the timelag which often occurs in the Federal Reserve's cheque collection process.

Flow of Funds
Analysis of the origin and use of funds in the different sectors of the economy.

Foreign Exchange
Claims to foreign currency payable abroad, including bank deposits, bills, cheques. Foreign exchange rates refer to the number of units of one currency needed to buy another.

Forward Book
Foreign exchange term for the total of net forward positions in various currencies, reflecting either current trading or a bank's view on a specific currency.

Forward Contract
Contract for settlement of foreign exchange transaction at any date later than spot.

Forward Cover
Arrangement by a purchaser or seller of foreign exchange to cover himself against unforeseen exchange rate movements through a forward foreign exchange contract.

Forward Exchange Rate
Rate at which a currency can be purchased or sold for delivery in the future.

Forward Forward
Simultaneous purchase and sale of one currency for different maturity dates in the forward market by means of:
(a) Contract providing for the future delivery of a deposit maturing on a further forward date. (b) Contract providing for the future delivery at a fixed price of a deposit maturing on a further forward date, i.e. creating a forward deposit.

Forward Intervention
Intervention by a central bank in forward markets aimed at influencing a currency's spot rate. It can also involve a central bank acting to influence forward interest rates in its currency.

Forward Margin
Discount or premium between the spot and forward rates for a currency.

Franc Zone
Currency zone grouping most former French West African colonies and French dependencies in the Pacific, coordinated and assisted by the Banque de France. It uses the CFA and CFP francs. See **CFA Franc** and **CFP Franc**.

Free (Open) Market
(a) Unrestricted movement of items in and out of a market, unhampered by tariffs or other trade barriers. (b) Market in which supply and demand fix prices without the influence of outside factors, i.e. government or central bank intervention. (c) Condition of trading that is not limited to any area or persons.

Free Reserves
Margin by which excess reserves exceed borrowings at Federal Reserve banks.

Freeze
Use of legislation or agreement to keep e.g. prices/wages at the levels prevailing when the freeze is introduced.

Frozen Assets
Assets, balances or credits temporarily blocked or frozen due to political circumstances, e.g. war, or legal action.

Fundamental Disequilibrium
Generally refers to a basic and serious imbalance in a country's balance of payments, thus providing justification

for devaluation or revaluation by a government under IMF rules governing exchange rate management.

G-5 See **Group of Five.**.

G-7 See **Group Of Seven.**

G-10 See **Group Of Ten.**

GAB See **General Arrangement to Borrow** under LENDING.

General Agreement On Tariffs and Trade (GATT) Established in Geneva in 1948 as a legislative and negotiating framework for international trade relations. It aims to minimise trade barriers, chiefly by eliminating quotas or reducing tariffs.

Generalised System of Preferences (GSP) Tariff cuts and quota increases intended to encourage exports from developing countries.

Gold Certificates See entry under COMMODITIES.

Gold Exchange Standard When a national currency cannot be used by residents to purchase gold from their central bank, and when the latter does not hold a large gold element in its reserve. Instead these reserves are held in the currency of a country allowing convertibility of its own currency into gold e.g. the US dollar until 1971. This is known as the gold exchange standard.

Gold Fix See entry under COMMODITIES.

Gold Franc Different gold francs are still used under various international agreements as a method of calculating assets and liabilities under these agreements, e.g. Poincaré franc for shipping. The balance sheet of the Bank for International Settlements (BIS) is defined in gold francs. The value of these gold francs used by the BIS is now expressed in terms of the SDR since there is no longer an official gold price. See **Special Drawing Rights (SDRs)**.

Gold Pool Agreement in 1961 among the central banks of Britain, Begium, France, Italy, Netherlands, West Germany, Swizerland and the USA intended to stabilise the gold price at close to the then official parity of 35 dollars an ounce. It broke up in 1968 after France renounced its membership in 1967.

Gold Reserves Gold bullion content of a central bank's monetary reserves.

Gold Standard Monetary system in which the gold value of a currency is fixed by law and the authorities, on demand, have to be prepared to exchange gold at a given rate for the currency. It was abandoned by most countries in the 1930s.

Gold Tranche First 25 per cent of a member country's quota with the IMF which had to be subscribed in gold though it might be less for new members with reserve difficulties. The remainder of the quota was in the member's domestic currency. A country could draw automatically, and without condition, on the IMF to the value of its gold tranche. See **Super Gold Tranche** and **International Monetary Fund** under LENDING.

Gramm-Rudman-Hollings Act US law named after its Senate sponsors, two Republicans and one Democrat respectively, requiring the gradual reduction of the federal budget deficit to a balanced budget by 1991.

Green Currency See entry under COMMODITIES.

Gross Domestic Product (GDP) Similar to Gross National Product but omits income from abroad.

Gross National Product (GNP) The total value of goods and services produced within a period of time by an economy, including government and private spending, fixed capital investment, net inventory change and net exports. Real GNP growth describes the increase in national output after subtracting inflation.

Gross National Product Deflator Method to establish the actual growth of goods and services by eliminating growth due to price increases. Normally expressed as a percentage and based on an index figure.

Gross National Product Gap Gap between actual real GNP and potential real GNP under full employment conditions. When the gap turns negative, an economy is said to be overheated.

Group Of Five (G-5) The more important members of the Group of Ten (G-10). These comprise the USA, Japan, West Germany, France and Britain.

Group Of Seven (G-7) Group of industrialised countries comprising of the Group of Five plus Canada and Italy. See **Group Of Five (G-5)** and **Group Of Ten (G-10)**.

Group Of Ten (G-10) Now joined by Switzerland, this group comprises 11 of the main industrialised countries within the framework of the IMF. Its aims is to create as stable a world economic system as possible by coordinating members' fiscal and monetary policies. Other members are Belgium, Britain, Canada, France, Italy, Japan, Netherlands, Sweden, United States and West Germany. Note: Austria has applied for membership.

Group Of 77 Actually comprises 127 countries and was established to help promote the views of developing countries on international trade and development in UNCTAD. Originally established with 77 countries. See **UNCTAD**.

Hard Currency	Strong currency, unencumbered by controls and easily exchangeable into other currencies.
Hoarding	Withdrawal of precious metals, coins and notes from active circulation for the purpose of accumulation without earning interest in anticipation of greater value, or profits in the future.
Hot Money	Sensitive short term speculative or arbitrage funds moving in very rapid response to exchange rate pressures or yield differentials.
Hyperinflation	Rapidly climbing, self fuelling inflation which may bring on economic collapse. See **Inflation**.
IADB	See **Inter-American Development Bank**.
IBEC	International Bank for Economic Cooperation. Established in 1964 to handle COMECON payments, especially transferable roubles. See **COMECON**.
ILO	International Labour Organisation. Its aim is to improve working conditions and social security throughout the world.
IMC	International Monetary Conference organised by the American Bankers' Association. Holds an important annual conference on financial and monetary questions. Those attending must be the chairman or chief executive of the member bank.
IMF	See **International Monetary Fund** under LENDING.
IMM	International Monetary Market. A division of the Chicago Mercantile Exchange (CME) for the trading of gold, foreign currencies and financial futures.
Import Cover	Number of months of gross imports whose cost would be covered by a country's monetary reserves.
Import Deposits	Method of import restrictions requiring importers to deposit a percentage of the value of their imports for a set time before it is repaid.
Import Duty	Tariff or customs tax levied on goods crossing a national border. Import surcharge is an additional duty.
Import Restrictions	Methods taken to reduce or control imports through a variety of measures including import deposits, licences or quotas. May be intended to correct a country's overall balance of payments deficit, or to protect a specific industrial sector.

Incomes Policy — Broad term covering the various direct forms of inflation control by a government which could include a freeze or limitation on increases in prices, wages, rents, dividends.

Indemnity — Guaranteed compensation against loss. Also security against contingent loss.

Indexation — System of linking wages, prices, interest rates etc. to a given index, thus producing in the former an automatic rise or decline.

Industrial Production Index — Coincident indicator measuring the physical output of manufacturing, mining and utility industries.

Inflation — Persistent upward movement in the general price level together with a related drop in purchasing power. Sometimes used to describe an excessive rate of such movement.

Info Rate — Foreign exchange and money market term used when a dealer is providing a rate for information purposes only and not for doing business. Indicative or Indication Rate sometimes used for the same purpose.

Inter-American Development Bank (IADB) — Set up in 1959 to provide development funds for Central and Latin American countries. As well as these states, Japan and a large number of European countries are members.

Interbank — See entry under LENDING.

Interest Parity — Occurs if the difference in interest rates on similar financial instruments in difference countries (e.g. US and UK three-month treasury bills) is reflected by the premium or discount on the relevant forward exchange rate.

Interim Committee — See entry under LENDING.

Internal Market — The European Community's goal of an EC-wide market without trade barriers or border controls to be completed by the end of 1992.

International Bank For Reconstruction And Development — See **World Bank** under LENDING.

International Chamber of Commerce (ICC) — Based in Paris this groups chambers of commerce, business and banking associations from around the world. It has an arbitration court used for settling international business disputes.

International Investment Bank	Set up in Moscow in 1971 to help finance development projects in the COMECON countries.
International Monetary Fund (IMF)	See entry under LENDING.
Internationalisation Of Currency	A currency is internationalised, if it is widely used to denominate trade and credit transactions by non-residents of the country of issue.
Intervention	(a) Central bank action in the open market to influence exchange rates, or to stabilise market conditions. See **Central Bank Intervention**. (b) Within the European Community intervention also refers to public purchasing of farm produce in order to support its market price at previously determined levels.
Intra-Day Limit	Limits allowed on a foreign exchange dealer's position in each and all currencies during the course of the trading day. Such limits may well be substantially larger than those allowed at the close of business, when books are squared as far as possible.
Investment	Employment of money in a purchase which is expected to produce an income or capital appreciation. Also anything which is purchased as a store of value.
Investment Currency	Exchange control system under which currency needed for the acquisition of foreign investment must be acquired through an investment currency market, unless exempted by special permission from the central bank. If the investment currency meets strong demand, it will sell at a high premium over the actual foreign exchange market rate for the currency.
Invisibles	Exports and imports of services as opposed to trade in physical goods or merchandise. They form part of the current balance of payments component, and include funds arising from shipping, tourism, insurance, banking and commodity services. See **Balance Of Payments**.
Islamic Banking	Banking based on adherence to Islamic principles, which prohibit usury. This is usually interpreted as forbidding the receipt or payment of interest. See **Usury**.
Islamic Development Bank	Based in Jeddah and set up in 1976, its role is the help finance development in countries with a substantial Islamic population.

'J' Curve   Graphic description of the initially perverse and then benign reaction of the balance of trade following devaluation. The trade balance deteriorates as import costs rise, then recovers to surplus as exports expand in volume due to cheaper exchange costs.

Jamaica Agreement   Meeting of the IMF Interim Committee in 1976 which led to the abolition of the official gold price, and produced new rules and guidelines for the exchange rate regime moving from a system of fixed rates on which IMF rules were based to one allowing for flexibility.

Jawbone   Rhetoric by a government or other body to influence economic decisions by business, banking, consumers and trade unions, usually accompanied by forecasts, and sometimes by policy warnings.

Kennedy Round   Round of industrial tariff cuts in GATT between 1964 and 1967, so called because the initiative came from President Kennedy's Trade Expansion Act.

Keynesian Economics   Body of economic thought developed by Britain's John Maynard Keynes and his followers based on a cause and effect analysis of the variations in aggregate spending and income. It stands in opposition to the view that the free market is the ultimate regulator and believes that economic performance could be improved by government intervention. See **Monetarism** and **Supply-Side Economics**.

Kondratieff Cycle   Named after the Russian economist Nikolai Kondratieff, who identified 50 to 60-year cycles of economic activity. Thus, it means a long lasting cycle.

Labour Force   Total number of employed and registered or estimated unemployed persons in the economy. The unemployment rate or jobless ratio is a percentage of the civilian labour force.

Lagging Indicator   Measure of economic activity that usually reaches a turning point of the business cycle after the overall economy has turned, e.g. GNP, consumer prices etc.

Latin American Reserve Fund   See **Andean Pact**.

Leading Indicator   Measure of economic activity that usually foreshadows peaks and troughs in total business, e.g. factory orders, stock prices.

Leads And Lags   Accelerated and decelerated foreign trade payments and receipts, usually associated with exchange rate speculation. In anticipation of a devaluation, payments for exports are delayed while the importer accelerates his payments.

Legal Tender   Means of payment which must be accepted by law in settlement of debt.

Less Developed Countries (LDCs)   Countries moving to a higher level of economic and social development. Commonly used to identify those countries which are not members of an established industrial grouping such as OECD, G-10, COMECON.

LIFFE   London International Financial Futures Exchange.

Link   (a) Relationship between trade and currency reform.
(b) Relationship between SDR allocations and development finance.

Louvre Accord   An agreement on currency stability reached in Paris in February 1987 by finance ministers of G-5 countries and Canada. The pact featured a unanimous call for a halt in the dollar's decline, and also detailed economic policies pledged by each participant to re-establish balanced trade and non-inflationary world economic growth. See **Group Of Five**.

Macro-Economics   Study of human activities in large groups as indicated by economic aggregates such as total employment, national income, investment, consumption, prices, wages and costs. See **Micro-Economics**.

Make-Up Day   Day when bank figures must be compiled for reporting to the central bank.

Managed Float   Currency float subject to guidance by discretionary central bank intervention. Also a dirty float, when intervention is deemed to delay unnecessarily needed government action, i.e. devaluation/revaluation, wage freeze.

Margin Requirements   (a) Incremental reserve obligations on credit instruments.
(b) In the USA, the percentage of reserves required by the Federal Reserve and exchanges to make an initial credit transaction or maintain a margin account.

Market Access   (a) Scope for access to a country's markets available to imported goods or commodities. (b) Access to a market for executing transactions.

Marketability   Measure of ease with which something can be bought and sold.

MATIF   The Paris financial futures market, Marché à Terme des Instruments Financiers. In autumn 1987 plans were announced to bring commodity futures under MATIF's supervision.

Medium Term Forecasts	Economic predictions ranging from seven quarters to four years ahead of the current period.
Micro-Economics	Study of the economic action of individual firms and well-defined small groups of individuals and sectors. See **Macro-Economics**.
Minimum Reserves	Minimum amount of reserves which commercial banks and other depository institutions are required to keep on deposit with a central bank. Sometimes called Registered Reserves.
Monetarism	School of economic thought which advocates strict control of the money supply as the major weapon of monetary policy, especially against inflation. Usually involves cuts in public spending and temporarily high interest rates. See **Keynesian Economics** and **Supply-Side Economics**.
Monetary Base	Monetary aggregate consisting of money held by the banks and public plus bank deposits with the central bank. Expansion of the monetary base is said to determine the potential growth rate of the broad money supply.
Monetary Policy	Management by a central bank of a country's money supply to ensure the availability of credit in quantities and at prices consistent with specific national objectives. The bank's tools include open market operations in the securities markets, intervention in foreign exchange and controls over financial institutions such as interest rate ceilings and curbs on lending. See **Fiscal Policy**.
Monetary Reform	Process of negotiating and drafting a revised international currency system.
Money Stock	Most frequently occurs as "Central Bank Money Stock", a measure of the West German money supply for which the Bundesbank set growth targets from 1975 until 1987. It consists of cash and banks' minimum reserves on domestic liabilities (calculated on the basis of the minimum reserve ratios applying in January 1974). These liabilities include sight deposits, time deposits and deposits with a statutory notice period. For 1988 the Bundesbank preferred to set growth targets for the broad-based money definition M3.
Money Supply	The total stock of money in an economy according to various definitions. The most narrowly defined version is M1, comprising cash and sight (demand in the USA) deposits with banks. Broader definitions (M2, M3 and M4) add in various categories of time and savings deposits and certificates of deposit until the broadest definition (M5) includes all that is deemed 'money' in the short, medium and long term. Britain also has M0, classed as a measure of the UK authorities' liabilities, covering notes and coins in

circulation and banks' operational balances with the Bank of England.

Moral Suasion
When central banks and governments try to influence market participants to do what they wish by persuasion rather than by coercion.

Most Favoured Nation (MFN)
An undertaking by two countries to give each other the maximum tariff concessions on their mutual trade which they already grant to other countries.

Multiple Exchange Rate
Use by a country of several exchange rates for different operations. Thus foreign investment, foreign tourists and raw material imports may be given a cheaper rate, while imports of non-essentials are charged with a higher rate of foreign exchange.

Multiplier
Conceptual tool referring to the magnified impact that investment and spending have on total income, or that reserve requirements have on bank positions.

Narrower Bands
Tighter exchange rate fluctuation margins than applied as a matter of standard international practice. See **Band**.

Nationalism (Of Currency)
This occurs when a central bank imposes restrictions on borrowing and lending of its currency by non-residents.

Net Liquidity Balance
US Department of Commerce term describing the overall balance of payments.

Non-Durables
Consumer or producer goods with a limited life.

Non-Tariff Barriers
Restrictive trade practices other than customs tariffs. Examples include import quotas, import licensing and price controls. See **Protectionism**.

NSCC
US National Securities Clearing Corp set up in 1977 by the merger of clearing facilities owned by the New York and American Stock Exchanges and the National Clearing Corp for the National Association of Securities Dealers.

NYFCC
New York Futures Clearing Corp set up by New York Futures Exchanges to handle clearing operations.

NYFE
New York Futures Exchange established in August 1979 and a wholly owned subsidiary of the New York Stock Exchange.

Odd Dates
Deals in foreign exchange and money markets for periods other than the regular market periods.

Official Journal
The Journal of the European Communities containing EC regulations, budgets, directives, decisions, opinions and recommendations.

Official Reserves
See **Reserves (Official)**.

Official Settlements Account
Also called reserves transactions account. A US balance of payments measure based on movements of dollars in foreign official holdings and in US reserves.

Organisation For Economic Cooperation And Development (OECD)
Established in 1961 to promote stable and sustainable economic growth in member countries and the expansion of world trade. Based in Paris. Members are the USA, Canada, Japan, Australia, New Zealand, all EC and EFTA members, and Turkey. Yugoslavia is an associate member.

Overhang
Involuntary foreign official holdings of a currency, usually a generalised condition, i.e. relating to a large number of countries and involving historically large amounts of the currency concerned net of working balances. The overhang represents in these circumstances temporary inconvertibility due to the inability of the reserve currency country to convert the overhang into other forms of acceptable reserve asset.

Overheated Economy
Often the result of high economic activity putting pressure on production capacity, causing interest rates to rise and fuel inflation. See **Gross National Product Gap**.

Overvalued
Situation where a market and economic conditions and pressures indicate a currency should be devalued. Opposite to **Undervalued**.

Paris
Foreign exchange term for the French Franc.

Paris Club
Informal group of government officials, representing western creditor nations and overseeing government-to-government loans, which have run into difficulties. Based in Paris, the club is run by the French Treasury.

Parity
Officially declared exchange rate in terms of SDR, gold or the US dollar. Also called Par Value.

Pegging
Term used to describe the end of a currency float and the setting of a fixed central rate or parity.

Petrodollars
Surplus funds resulting from oil sales for dollars by oil producing countries.

Planned Economy
Economy where distribution of resources is centrally controlled by the government.

Plaza Accord   Agreement reached in September 1985 by Group of Five nations to lower the value of the dollar. Their meeting took place in New York's Plaza Hotel. See **Louvre Accord.**

Potential GNP   Output that an economy can produce when operating at full employment capacity.

Premium   See entry under GENERAL MARKET TERMS.

Primary Reserves   Gold-related monetary reserves, i.e. gold, SDR, reserve position in the IMF.

Prior Import Deposits   Import deposits which need to be paid before an import licence is granted.

Producer Price Index   See **Wholesale Price Index.**

Productivity   Output per man-hour or unit of capital.

Protectionism   Imposition of border taxes (customs duties) on imports in order to protect a domestic industry from cheaper competitive products. But it can also encompass import restrictions or export subsidies. Some countries employ non-tariff forms of protectionism such as certain health and environmental regulations relating to imports.

Protectionism (Of The Currency)   Central bank system to protect currency with restrictions in order to move the exchange rate in a direction consistent with the economic policies of the government concerned.

Pump Priming   Government expenditure to stimulate a business recovery and achieve full employment.

Quota   (a) Quantitative limit on imports or exports. May be applied to a specific product or general group of products from a single country or a group of countries. (b) Production target, or limit on production. (c) Country's subscription to the IMF. 25 per cent used to be represented by gold (now by SDRs) and the remainder by a subscription in the country's domestic currency. The size of the country's quota governs its voting rights within the IMF.

Regal GNP   True level of national output after subtracting inflation.

Real Income/ Wage   Personal spending power or true wages received after adjusting for inflation.

Recession   Decline in overall business activity, classically defined as two consecutive quarterly falls in real GNP. See **Depression.**

Re-Export	Export of imported goods or commodities without substantial processing or transformation.
Reflation	The administered recovery of an economy, ideally by boosting demand without fuelling inflation. Also a type of inflation during a recovery period in which prices are restored to a desirable previous gradient by monetary policy.
Regulations (EC)	Acts of the EC council of Ministers or the Commission which are totally binding and directly applicable in all member states.
Reserve Currency	Currency which is internationally acceptable and is used by central banks to meet their financial commitments abroad.
Reserves (Official)	Official foreign exchange reserves kept to ensure a government can meet current and near term claims. Official reserves are an asset in a country's balance of payments.
Retail Price Index (RPI)	Measurement of the monthly change in the average level of prices at the retail level. It does not normally cover luxury goods.
Revaluation	Upward adjustment of a currency's parity or central rate. Revaluation results from a decision by the relevant authorities. If a currency moves upwards in market trading, this is called **appreciation**. See **Devaluation**.
Safeguard	Temporary action to protect domestic economy from a flood of imports.
Savings Ratio	Percentage of disposable personal income that is saved or used to repay debt.
SDR	See **Special Drawing Right**.
Seasonal Adjustment	Statistical allowance for seasonal monthly or quarterly swings in the raw data of an economic series. (Annual rate figures have no adjustment factor since the seasonal influence is no longer relevant.) Some key series such as employment, retail sales and money supply have much seasonal variation.
SELA	Caracas-based Latin American Economic System (SELA) coordinates economic policy in the region and cooperates on technology, food etc.
Settlements	Inter-central bank payments to cover external deficits and intervention debts.
SITC	Standard International Trade Classification. A uniform system of presenting and reporting trade statistics.

Slump	Severe or sustained stagnation in overall economic activity.
Smithsonian Agreement	Agreement of December 18, 1971 among the Group of Ten on major parity adjustments which included a devaluation of the US dollar against gold, a widening of parity bands to 2.25 per cent either side of par from one per cent, and the suspension of a 10 per cent US import surcharge.
Smithsonian Rates	Exchange rates fixed by the Smithsonian Agreement by the Group of Ten signatories and subsequently by non-participating countries.
Sovereign Immunity	Legal doctrine which provides that in certain cases a sovereign state cannot be sued or have its assets seized.
Spare Capacity	Margin of unused manufacturing capacity in an economy or company.
Special Drawing Rights (SDRs)	Created by the International Monetary Fund in 1969 as an international reserve asset to supplement existing reserve assets. The IMF uses SDRs for book-keeping purposes. In January 1981, it reduced the number of currencies in its SDR currency basket from 16 to the five most widely traded currencies, each with a specific weighting, (these are the US dollar, mark, sterling, yen and French franc). SDRs can be used for a variety of purposes among holders, including loans, swap arrangements and forward operations.
Squeeze	Official action by a central bank or government to reduce supply in order to force up the price of money. See entry under COMMODITIES.
Stagflation	Recession, stagnation or severe growth slowdown that is accompanied by steep inflation.
Sterilisation	Process by which a central bank acts to neutralise the impact on domestic liquidity of its currency market intervention. For example, if the bank sells its national currency to brake that currency's rise, it may reduce a growth in money supply by selling bonds to mop up the extra liquidity which it has created.
Stop Go	Economic policy alternating periods of economic restriction and expansion.
Structural Unemployment	Unemployment resulting from a basic underlying change in the economy or a specific industry.
Super Gold Tranche	Automatic drawing right with the IMF represented by reductions below 75 per cent of quota of the fund's holdings of a given currency. The member country can obtain funds if needed to the full amount represented by the super gold

tranche without incurring any conditions. See **International Monetary Fund** under LENDING.

Supply-Side Economics
Proponents believe tax cuts will boost investment in production and increase the supply of goods in the economy. They believe policy makers should focus on the need to encourage supply, whereas Keynesians concentrate on controlling demand. See **Monetarism** and **Keynesian Economics**.

Taft-Hartley Act
Primary law in US labour management relations endowing the executive branch of government with substantial powers to prevent and settle labour disputes, such as the imposition of cooling-off periods, usually 90 days, and the determination of collective bargaining procedures.

Tariff
Customs duty or border tax levied on imports. See **Non-Tariff Barriers**.

Terms Of Trade
Relationship between export and import price indices. If export prices rise more quickly, or fall at a slower pace than import prices, there is a favourable ratio.

Tight Money
Monetary restraint policy restricting the availability of credit and usually forcing interest rates higher. See **Easy Money**.

Tom/Next
Tomorrow/next. Simultaneous purchase of a currency for delivery the next business day and for the spot day or vice versa.

Trade Barrier
Artificial restraint on the free exchange of goods and services between countries, usually in the form of tariffs, subsidies, quotas or exchange controls.

Trade Deficit/ Surplus
Excess of imports over exports (deficit) or vice versa for a surplus.

Treaty Of Rome
Founding treaty of the EC. Signed in Rome on March 25, 1957 by the six founding members to set up the European Economic Community from January 1, 1958. See **European Communities**.

Two-Tier Market
Dual exchange rate system under which one tier is openly responsive to market pressure and the other is insulated by government intervention or control. E.g. Belgian financial and convertible francs.

UNCTAD
United Nations Conference on Trade and Development. Established in 1964 to promote better international trading conditions for developing countries and to help raise their standard of living. It is also a forum for most commodity price stabilisation pacts.

Undervalued	See **Overvalued**.
Unified Budget	US budgetary format covering receipts and outlays for Federal and trust funds after deducting the transactions that flow between them.
Unit Of Account	(a) A monetary unit widely used in the EC until 1979 and valued at one pre-Smithsonian dollar. It was then superseded for most transactions including agriculture, by the European Currency Unit (ECU). (b) A composite unit used to denominate some Eurobond issues or any hypothetical composite unit of currency measurement, e.g. SDRs.
Unitary Wage Rate	Average hourly wage rate paid to a blue-collar worker in US manufacturing industry.
Usury	Charging of excessive or unreasonable rates of interest. See **Islamic Banking**.
Variable (Import) Levy	Customs duty rate which varies in response to some internal price criterion.
VAT	Value Added Tax. System of taxing products on the amount of value added at each stage of their production and exchange.
Velocity Of Money	Rate at which a unit of money is used within a given time. It is usually measured as the ratio of gross national product to the money stock. An increase in the velocity of money can reduce the effectiveness of a restrictive monetary policy.
Visible Balance (Of Trade)	Country's trade in exports and imports of merchandise goods. See **Invisibles**.
Wage Drift	Difference between basic wages and actual earnings, usually reflecting overtime, bonus payments etc.
Wage Indexation	Fully or partially adjusting wages in line with inflation.
Weekly Return	Series of statistics issued weekly e.g. summarising balance sheet position of most central banks.
Wholesale Price Index (WPI)	Wholesale prices are calculated as products move through the manufacturing and distribution stage before they go on sale to consumers. The WPI typically anticipates movements in the consumer price index by two or three months. Usually divided into foods and industrial products.
Working Balance	Discretionary currency component of a central bank's overall monetary reserves.

Lending

AAA

Top rating for bonds (primarily US corporate and municipal) of the highest quality awarded by Standard and Poor's or by Moody's, the two principal American rating companies. An AAA issuer is viewed as least likely to miss payments on principal and interest. See **Credit Rating, Moody's** and **Standard and Poor's**.

Acceleration Clause

A feature of convertible notes or bonds that allows the borrower to call the issue early if the market price of a stock exceeds the conversion price by a specified amount over a specified period (e.g. by 150 per cent for 30 consecutive days).

Acceptance Credit

An exporter or importer may obtain funds from a bank arranging for it to accept bills of exchange drawn on it by him. The bills can then be sold, as the bank's acceptance means the buyer of the bills can look to the bank for payment.

Acceptance House

Financial institution lending money on the security of bills of exchange. It may lend money on a bill or add its name to a bill drawn on another party, especially in foreign trade. Acceptance houses often lend money to an exporter to cover the gap between the production of goods and the receipt of proceeds from their sale. The loan is made through a bill of exchange and is sometimes called an acceptance credit.

Accepting Houses Committee

The 17 leading London merchant banks. Bills of exchange drawn on them are discountable at fine rates. The committee also ensures policy co-ordination between its members, the Treasury and the Bank of England.

Acceptor

Drawee who signs a bill of exchange and thereby undertakes to pay the bill at its maturity.

Accretion

Addition of principal or interest to a fund over a period as the result of an accumulation plan. In portfolio accounting, discount bonds are accreted at par, while premium bonds are amortised to par.

Accrued Interest

Interest due from issue or from the most recent coupon date to the present on an interest bearing security. If the security is sold, the price is adjusted to take into account accrued interest.

ACH

Automated Clearing House. A US computer based clearing and settlement operation often operated by a Federal Reserve bank, established for the exchange of electronic (i.e.

paperless) transactions among participating depository institutions.

Advance Refunding Extension of public debt before maturity.

Advisory Funds Funds placed with a bank or other financial institution to invest at its own discretion on the client's behalf.

After Sight Bill of exchange drawn after sight is payable when it has been accepted and the acceptor has written an acceptance date on the bill.

After Market Trading of bonds immediately after issue.

Afterdate A bill of exchange payable at a certain time after the date of the bill.

Agency Bank Form of organisation frequently used by foreign banks to enter the US market. An agency bank is unable to accept deposits or extend loans in its own name. It acts as agent for the parent bank.

Agent Bank Bank appointed by members of an international lending syndicate to protect the lenders' interests during the life of a loan. Similar to the trustee of a bond issue.

Agreement Amongst Underwriters Legal document binding an underwriting group into a syndicate. In the USA it is normally between the borrower (issuer) and all the underwriters. In the UK and Eurobond markets it may be limited to an agreement between managing underwriters, who then make sub-underwriting agreements with other underwriters.

AIBD Association of International Bond Dealers, the Zurich-based self-regulatory body which represents the primary and secondary Eurobond markets.

Allotment See the entry under EQUITIES.

Amortisation Gradual redemption of a debt through a periodic repayment of principal and interest. Often includes use of a sinking fund. See **Sinking Fund**.

Applied Proceeds Swap Proceeds from the sale of a block of bonds in the USA which are then used in buying another block of bonds.

Approved Securities Securities or obligations of states etc., which are approved for holding by banks and financial institutions as part of their reserves or similar requirements.

Asian Dollar Bonds Similar to Eurobonds, but based in Singapore. The market emerged following the successful development of the Asian dollar market. See **Eurobond**.

Asian Dollars US dollar bank deposits normally held in Asia and traded outside the USA, similar to Eurodollars. The market is based in Singapore.

As Per Advice Indicates the drawee of a bill of exchange has been notified that the bill has been drawn on him.

At Call Money or funds at call, i.e. immediately available.

At Sight A bill of exchange payable on presentation rather than on a specific date.

Authority To Purchase/ Negotiate Used especially in trade with the Far East. A bill is drawn on the buyer and presented with shipping documents to the London bank acting for the purchaser's bank. If the documents are in order, the London bank buys the bill from the exporter.

Ausfuhrkredit GmbH (AKA) Export credit company formed by a consortium of all West German commercial banks to provide medium and long term export finance.

Aval Payment of a bill of exchange or a promissory note which is guaranteed by the signature of a third person on the bill. European term.

Average Life Maturity of a borrowing after taking into account repayments or purchases by the borrower's sinking fund.

Back to Back Credit Credit opened by a finance house or bank on the strength of another credit and used in foreign trade. The foreign importer provides the finance house with the relevant documents, on the strength of which a credit is opened in favour of the exporter. These can then be used to back another credit for the exporter, i.e. the first credit backs the second.

Back to Back Loan Arrangement whereby a loan in the currency of one country is set against a loan in another country's currency. It can be used to avoid or overcome exchange risks and controls, although interest rate differentials may cause problems.

Backing Support Gold or silver securities used to support a state's note issue.

Balloon Loan where the last repayment is much larger than the other repayments, or where the loan is repaid at maturity.

Bank Bill Bill of exchange issued or accepted by a bank. It is thus more acceptable than a normal trade bill of exchange as the risk is less, while the discount is also smaller.

Bank Deposit
Money held by a bank on behalf of a private, corporate, banking or government customer. It appears in the bank's accounts as a liability.

Bank Rate
Official discount rate set by a central bank. See **Discount Rate**. Sometimes refers to the interest rate charged by a commercial bank on typical loans.

Bank Release
Issued by a bank after being paid on a bill of exchange and enables the purchaser of the goods to take delivery.

Bankers Acceptance
Negotiable time draft drawn on and accepted by a bank which adds its credit to that of an importer of merchandise. It typically arises from letters of credit in foreign trade. The posted rate is an indicated rate that many foreign banks use to finance letters of credit. It is not a real indication of the rates in the dealer market and is used as a rate for small transactions. The bank offered rate is the rate at which the bank is willing to transact business in the market.

Bankers Draft
Draft payable on demand and drawn by or on behalf of the bank itself. It is regarded as cash and cannot be returned unpaid. Often used in international trade.

Bardepot
West German regulation which requires a percentage of foreign borrowings by German residents to be deposited in cash in a non-interest bearing account with the Bundesbank.

Base Rate
Annual interest rate on which graduated lending charges are calculated by British banks.

Basis Point
Unit of measurement (usually one hundredth of a percentage point or 0.01 per cent) typically used in expressing bond yield differentials. Thus, 7.50 per cent - 7.15 per cent = 0.35 per cent or 35 basis points. See entry under GENERAL MARKET TERMS.

Bearer Bond
Bond in which ownership is transferable to the bearer, rather than registered on the books of the issuer in the name of a particular person. Bearer securities normally have a coupon attached to them which is detached as interest payments become due, and is presented as evidence of the bearer's right to payment.

"Big Bank" Syndicate
A Swiss bond-issuing syndicate, led by Union Bank of Switzerland, Crédit Suisse and Swiss Bank Corp, which issues a majority of new Swiss franc bonds.

Bill Broker
Firm or individual who buys and sells bills of exchange. The term is interchangeable with a discount house in the UK.

Blocked Accounts Bank accounts where payment cannot be freely made, e.g. accounts frozen for political reasons.

Bill of Exchange Key negotiable instrument of exchange in international trade. It is an unconditional order in writing addressed by one person to another, signed by the person giving it, requiring the person to whom it is addressed to pay on demand, or at a fixed or determinable future time, a certain sum in money to, or to the order of, a specified person or the bearer.

Bond Usually a fixed interest security under which the issuer contracts to pay the lender a fixed principal amount at a stated date in the future, and a series of interest payments, either semi-annually or annually. Interest payments may vary through the life of a bond. Issuers include government, municipal and corporate entities. Bonds maturing in less than five years are described as short term, between six and 15 years as medium term, and more than 15 years as long term. In the USA a bond is normally for more than 10 years. See **Debenture**.

Bond Anticipatory Notes (BANs) Notes issued in the USA by states and municipalities to provide interim finance for projects to be funded by bond issues.

Bond Indenture Legal document in the USA setting out the duties of the issuer and the rights of the holder.

Bond Market Primary or secondary market for government municipal or corporate debt securities. See **Primary** and **Secondary Market**.

Bond Yield Rate of annual income return on a bond expressed as a percentage of its price. There are three types of yield—nominal, current, and yield to maturity.

Borrowing Requirement Net amount of money needed by a government to finance budget deficits and maturing debt.

Bought Deal A new issue procedure whereby a lead manager, acting on its own or together with a syndicate, commits to buy an entire securities issue on fixed terms.

Bracket Term used in the USA and Euromarkets to group the different categories of managers, and underwriters of syndicated loans. The lead manager, co-manager, top underwriter, major underwriters etc. are listed alphabetically within their respective brackets.

Bridge Financing Interim financing.

Broadcast System of syndicating Eurocredits by offering widespread participation by telex/letter to potential lending institutions.

Buffer Stock Financing Facility   See entry under COMMODITIES.

Bulldog Bond   Bond denominated in sterling issued by a non-UK resident in the UK market.

Bullet Bond   Bond, usually a Eurobond, which has no early redemption, i.e. is redeemed at full maturity.

Bundesobligation   Savings bond or medium term note issued on an ongoing basis over an extended period in different series by the West German Federal government and traded in a secondary market. They cannot be bought by foreigners.

Buono Ordinario Del Tesoro (BOT)   Italian Treasury bills with maturities of three, six or 12 months.

Buono Del Tesoro Poliennale (BTP)   Polyannual, i.e. medium-term, fixed-rate Italian Treasury bill with maturities of more than 12 months.

Busted Convertible   US term for a convertible issue which is virtually worthless, as the value of the supporting stock has fallen sharply.

Buy Back   See **Repurchase Agreement**.

Buyer Credit   Export financing arrangement under which a foreign buyer raises a loan from a bank to pay an exporter.

Calendar   Timetable or schedule, official or otherwise, of future new securities issues on domestic and international capital markets.

Call Feature   The optional right of an issuer to redeem bonds before their stated maturity at a given price on a given date: also, a contract allowing the holder to buy a given number of securities from the issuer of such a contract at a fixed price for a given period of time.

Call Loan   Commercial bank loan repayable on demand by the lender and repayable at any time by the borrower.

Call Money   Interest bearing deposits which are repayable at call, i.e. on demand. Covers both domestic money market and Euromarket funds. Also known as day to day money or demand money.

Call Price   Price at which a US bond issue can be called, usually at par or a slight premium.

Call Rate   Rate of interest payable on call money.

Callable Bond

Bond which can be redeemed before maturity by the payment of a specified call price. This can help the borrower in cases when interest rates have fallen since the bond offering.

Capital Exports

Outflow of funds from the capital account, i.e. those items not included in a country's current account balance of payments, including investment and deposit funds, aid and military expenditure. If these exports are substantial over a short period of time, they are referred to as a capital flight.

Capital Market

Market for loanable funds. Usually used when referring to medium and long term finance, while the money market is more involved with short term debt.

Cash Management Bill

Very short term US Treasury bills with one to 20 days maturity and designed to maintain balances until taxes are received.

CEDEL

Centrale de Livraison de Valeurs Mobilières, Luxembourg. A computerised clearing system for Eurobonds. See **Euroclear**.

Central Government Borrowing Requirement (CGBR)

Difference in the UK between the government's expenditure and revenue, excluding the local authority sector. When it includes local authorities, it become the Public Sector Borrowing Requirement (PSBR).

Certificate of Deposit (CD)

Interest bearing negotiable time deposit of fixed maturity at a commercial bank. The posted rate is an indicated rate at which the bank is willing to take on the deposit. However, a bank will negotiate a rate with a larger depositor.

Certificato Di Credito Del Tesoro (CCT)

A long term variable interest rate credit certificate issued by the Italian Treasury.

Club

General distribution of tasks within a group of banks involved in loan syndication on the Euromarkets. It eschews the traditional system of designating lead managers, co-managers etc. May also refer to governmental arrangements for rescheduling debt. See **Paris Club** under ECONOMY, CURRENCY.

Co-Financing

Finance jointly provided for a country by commercial banks and international financing institutions, such as the IMF, World Bank or regional development banks. It is one way of effectively increasing the amount lent by international institutions. The terms, which they insist on for ensuring the loan conditions are observed, reassure commercial banks concerned over the possible security of their own loans. The banks are thus more willing to lend.

Collateralised Mortgage Obligations (CMOs)	Bonds backed by a pool of mortgages held by the issuer. The principal cash flows of the pool are channelled sequentially into tranches of bonds. Interest is semi-annual. Usually, coupon payments are not made on the final tranche until after redemption of the other tranches and interest is added to the principal. This tranche is called an accretion or accrual bond.
Co-Manager	In securities issues, usually an invitee on an ad hoc basis either by the lead manager or at the request of the issuer of the securities or guarantor. Usually between two and 10 co-managers share responsibility, chiefly for pricing and placement. As a rule co-managers make larger underwriting commitments than do syndicate participants.
Commercial Paper	In the US domestic market, a promissory note or draft of a corporation, government agency or bank holding company, usually unsecured but backed by unused bank credit lines and issued for short term credit needs. It normally has a maturity of up to 270 days and is usually sold at a discount from face value. Directly placed paper is sold by the issuer directly to the investor while dealer placed paper is sold to an intermediary who in turn reoffers it to investors. Many companies have the capability to sell directly and there is a slight yield advantage in directly placing the paper. In the UK, a domestic market for sterling commercial paper has slightly different rules.
Commissioned Bank	Unique to the Japanese capital market, it combines the roles of trustee and paying agent for bond issues.
Commitment Fee	Fee charged by banks on the unused portion of a loan.
Commodity Credit Corporation (CCC)	See entry under COMMODITIES.
Communal Bond	A bond issued by a West German mortgage bank or public sector bank and secured by a loan to the public sector.
Compensation Balance	Amount of a commercial loan, usually expressed as a percentage of the loan which the borrower is required to keep on deposit with the bank.
Compensatory Financing	IMF facility providing short term finance to compensate for fluctuations in a country's export levels caused by circumstances largely outside a country's control.
Conditionality	Conditions imposed when a country draws funds from the IMF related to its credit tranches. There are four tranches and borrowing under each tranche attracts its own

conditions. Other conditions apply to borrowing beyond regular credit tranches such as where a country borrows to replace finance lost through a decline in exports. See **Compensatory Financing**.

Contract Financing
Finance for projects which use a commercial contract as security.

Conversion Issue
New issue of bonds timed to correspond with a maturing issue by the same borrower. The offering is structured in such a way that investors are given an incentive to exchange or convert the old issue into the new one.

Conversion Premium
Premium paid to redeem outstanding bonds before maturity.

Conversion Price
The share price at which the principal amount of a convertible bond may be used to acquire shares in or owned by the issuing company or shares in a related company.

Conversion Ratio
Number of shares which may be acquired upon the conversion of a convertible bond. The ratio is calculated as the bond principal amount divided by the conversion price.

Convertible Bond
Bond that can be converted, on the holder's option, into the shares of the issuing company, or its parent company, usually within a specified time.

Convertible FRN
Floating rate note which is convertible into a fixed rate bond, usually at the option of the investor.

Country Risk
Risk of lending funds to or making an investment in a particular country.

Coupon
Interest rate payable on bearer, and sometimes registered, securities especially bonds. It also means the detachable certificate entitling the bearer to payment of the interest.

Cover
Collateral deposited as security against borrowing.

Covered Warrant
Certificate which entitles an investor to buy securities or other assets at a given exercise price during a certain period of time. "Covered" because the securities or assets have been set aside for the potential exercise of the warrant. See **Naked Warrant** and **Warrant**.

Credit Rating
Overall credit-worthiness of a borrower. In the USA the two rating agencies are Moody's and Standard and Poor's. A top rating is described as "triple A" or "AAA", meaning there is thought to be almost no risk of the borrower failing to pay interest and principal. As the rating grade falls, the perceived risk grows. See **Moody's** and **Standard and Poor's**.

Credit Risk   Risk that a borrower may default on his obligations; a danger that interest payments and repayment of principal will not occur.

Creditor Nation   Country with a balance of payments surplus. Opposite to **Debtor Nation**.

Cross Currency   When a corporation's debt service needs in a given currency
Exposure   are not covered by a revenue, or potential revenue, in that currency.

Cross Default   Clause in a loan agreement stipulating that default by the borrower on any other loans will be regarded as a default on the loans governed by that clause.

Cum Coupon   The situation where the purchaser of a bond is entitled to receive the next interest payment. (See entry under EQUITIES.) Opposite is **Ex Coupon**.

Currency Option   Allows payment of principal and interest on a Eurobond
Clause   issued in one currency to be made in a different currency at the option of the purchaser.

Current Coupon   The prevailing coupon on a floating rate note or other variable rate security.

Current Yield   A measurement of the return to a bondholder calculated as the ratio of coupon to market price expressed as a percentage. See entry under EQUITIES.

Daimyo Bonds   Japanese bearer bonds considered more liquid than Samurai issues, because they can be settled by such European clearing organisations as Cedel or Euroclear. See **Samurai Bond**.

Dated Date   Date from which interest begins to accrue on a new US bond issue.

Dated Securities   Securities with a fixed redemption date. Long dated securities indicate redemption is a long way off.

Dealer Loan   Overnight loan to a dealer, backed by collateral.

Debenture   A written acknowledgement of a debt; a bond. In the USA a debenture whether straight or convertible is secured by a general guarantee and not by a lien on specific assets, while bonds are unsecured. In the UK a debenture is usually secured by a charge on corporate assets, while bonds are unsecured.

Debt Management   Manipulation of three aspects of government debt: the level of interest rates, the pattern of ownership and the maturity schedule.

Debt Service Ratio

(a) Cost to a country of servicing its foreign debts and, in particular, debts owed by the public sector and publicly guaranteed debt. The cost comprises the total of interest payments and repayments of principal as a percentage of export earnings. A level of 20 per cent is normally considered an acceptable maximum, but accurately establishing the exact figure is often difficult. (b) The ratio of debt to equity in a commercial enterprise. It thus helps to measure a company's financial stability and its ability to increase its level of total borrowings.

Debtor Nation

Country with a balance of payments deficit, the opposite of **Creditor Nation**.

Default

If a borrower does not repay either the interest or the principal according to the conditions governing the loan, he is in default. In certain cases the creditors may consent to a rescheduling of the payments to avoid default. See **Repayment** and see entry under COMMODITIES.

Deficit Financing

Budgetary policy which produces a deficit and hence a government borrowing requirement. It can be the direct result of positive governmental action or of a failure to control spending.

Demand Deposit

Bank deposit that can be withdrawn without prior notice. Also called a sight deposit.

Direct Paper

Commercial paper sold direct by the issuer to investors.

Direct Placement

Placing of a new issue directly, usually with institutional investors, rather than through an underwritten offering.

Discount

The difference between present and maturity value, or the action of buying financial paper at less than par value before maturity. See entry under GENERAL MARKET TERMS.

Discount Bond

Bond selling below par almost always in the secondary market.

Discount Market

UK domestic money market. Financial houses dealing in this money market as well as in Treasury bills and bills of exchange are called discount houses.

Discount Rate

Interest rate at which a central bank will discount government paper or lend money against government paper collateral. In the USA it is the rate at which the Federal Reserve will lend short term funds to depository institutions.

Discount Securities — Money market instruments issued at a discount and redeemed at maturity for all the full face value, e.g. Treasury bills.

Discount Window — In the USA a lending facility provided by the Federal Reserve to eligible depository institutions.

Disintermediation — Placing of funds directly in securities by investors in a switch away from banks or other financial intermediaries which then place the funds in the credit market.

Documentary Credit — Used in financing foreign trade. It may be confirmed or unconfirmed, revocable or irrevocable. It provides an exporter with immediate payment, while giving an importer credit.

Domestic Credit Expansion (DCE) — In the UK the **Public Sector Borrowing Requirement (PSBR)** minus sales of public sector debt to the non-bank private sector plus the increase in bank lending to the private and overseas sectors.

Double Call — Sinking fund arrangement giving borrowers an obligation to redeem a fixed number of bonds annually, possibly double the amount due for redemption in that year.

Drawdown — Means to take up funds made available from financial institutions. It can include credits from the International Monetary Fund, Eurocredits from banks or a corporate utilisation of a credit granted by a domestic bank.

Drawing — Drawing the number of securities (bonds) to be redeemed by lot.

Droplock Loan — Medium term floating rate facility that automatically becomes a fixed rate bond if interest rates fall to a pre-determined level. For example, a loan with interest of 0.75 per cent over London interbank offered rates (Libor) could become a fixed rate bond with 13.50 per cent interest if, say, yields on government bonds fell below 12.75 per cent.

Dual-Currency Bond — A bond, seen particularly on the Swiss franc market, which is issued and pays interest in one currency but is redeemable in another currency.

Due Bill — In the USA an instrument establishing the obligation of a seller to deliver securities to the purchaser. A bill of exchange falling due for payment.

Edge Act — US 1919 act allowing US banks to form subsidiaries to carry out international banking business in the USA. Such subsidiaries can operate outside the state in which the parent bank is based.

Either/Or Facility Arrangement allowing a US concern to borrow Eurodollars from a foreign branch or dollars from the bank's head office.

Eligible Bankers Acceptance In the USA a bankers acceptance may be "eligible" if it can be sold by the accepting bank without creating a reserve requirement, or if the Federal Reserve will accept it as collateral at the discount window.

Eligible Bills/ Paper Bills or paper which are eligible for rediscount at the Bank of England.

Equipment Trust Certificate Security or bond issued (mainly in the USA) to pay for new equipment, and secured on the equipment. Ownership is held by a trustee until the debt is repaid. Used to purchase aircraft, railway equipment etc.

Equivalent Bond Yield A US measure to assess the true annual yield on a short term non-interest bearing security bought on a discount basis. It is used to compare Treasury bill nominal returns with yields on securities.

Eurobond International straight or convertible bond issued by state or corporate entities, denominated in a Eurocurrency, and issued outside the currency's domicile.

Euroclear Computerised clearing system for Eurobonds operated and managed under contract by the Brussels branch of Morgan Guaranty Trust Co of New York. See **CEDEL**.

Eurocredit Medium term international credits in a Eurocurrency usually provided by a syndicate of banks. Such credits are normally for a fixed term with an agreed margin, and base rate, e.g. the London interbank offered rate (Libor) for six month deposits in the Eurocurrency being used.

Eurocurrency Bank deposit made and held outside the country of the currency's domestic origin, e.g. Euromarks, Euro French francs, Euro Swiss francs, Euroyen etc.

Eurodollars Most extensively used Eurocurrency. It is a US dollar held by a non-resident of the USA, usually in the form of a deposit with a commercial bank outside America, including deposits at foreign branches of US banks.

Euromarket Overall term for international capital markets dealing in Eurobonds, Eurocredits etc.

Euronote Short term notes issued on a three to six month basis in the syndicated market, usually structured as a medium term loan in which the underwriters agree to issue notes on request.

Eurosyndicated Loans　Large bank credits, usually with maturities of three to 10 years granted by international bank syndicates put together on an ad hoc basis. Lenders are almost exclusively banks and finance companies, thus these credits are not placed with private investors. Interest rates are calculated by adding a margin to interbank offered rates and usually adjusted every three to six months. Funds for the loans are drawn from the Euromarket.

Evergreen Credit　Revolving credit with no fixed maturity date, which a bank has the option once annually to convert into a term loan.

Extendible　Eurobond security which gives the investor the option of extending its initial maturity for a given number of years. If the option is not exercised, the bond is repaid at the earlier maturity. Extensions are also possible on some short-term Eurolending facilities.

Ex Coupon　Without taking into account the coupon, i.e. if a bond is sold ex coupon, the seller will not receive the payment due on the coupon. Opposite is **Cum Coupon**.

Exempt Securities　Securities in the USA which are exempt from certain Securities and Exchange Commission registration and margin requirements. These include government, agency and municipal securities as well as commercial paper and private placements.

Exposure　When a bank provides funds to a country or corporation, it becomes exposed to the borrower. Most banks have internal rules designed to prevent overexposure to any single borrower. See entry under ECONOMY, CURRENCY.

Extended Fund Facility (EFF)　Assistance provided to IMF member countries with economies suffering from serious balance of payments difficulties due to structural imbalances in production, trade and prices or economies characterised by slow growth and an inherently weak balance of payments position. Drawings can be made over a period of three years under conditions similar to IMF standby drawings.

Face Value　Apparent worth. The nominal value which appears on the face of a document recording an entitlement, generally a certificate or bond. For indebtedness, the amount to be repaid at maturity.

Facility Fee　Charge paid by borrowers to banks for the extension of a credit facility.

Factoring　Service which enables a company to collect money on credit sales. The factor purchases the company's invoiced debts for cash but at a discount, and then seeks repayment from the original purchaser of the company's goods or services.

Federal Credit Agencies

US Federal government sponsored agencies providing credit to different groups of institutions and persons. Many are privately owned.

Federal Deposit Insurance Corp (FDIC)

Established in the USA in 1933 to insure accounts at commercial and mutual savings banks and thus protect depositors. All Federal Reserve members are required to be members. It has Federal supervisory authority over insured state banks not members of the Federal Reserve.

Federal Financing Bank

Obtains funds from the US Treasury for lending for Federal credit agencies.

Federal Funds

Reserve balances that US depository institutions lend each other, usually on an overnight basis. Federal Funds also include some other kinds of borrowings by depository institutions from each other and federal agencies. The funds are regarded as a key indicator of all US domestic interest rates.

Federal Home Loans Banks (FHLB)

Comprise 12 US banks and the FHLB board. They oversee the operations of all Federal savings and loan associations and federally insured state chartered Savings and Loans as well as providing finance. See **Savings and Loan Association**.

Federal National Mortgage Association (FNMA)

Or Fannie Mae. A US government-sponsored corporation owned entirely by private stockholders. It purchases and sells residential mortgages. Purchases of mortgages are financed by the sale of corporate obligations to private investors. See **Government National Mortgage Association (GNMA)**.

Federal Open Market Committee (FOMC)

This 12-member policy committee of the US Federal Reserve system meets periodically to set Federal Reserve guidelines, followed by the Federal Reserve Bank of New York's open market desk in buying and selling government securities in the open market as a means of influencing the volume and cost of bank credit and money. The FOMC also establishes policy relating to operations in the foreign exchange markets.

Fed Wire

The US Federal Reserve's electronic communications system (See **Federal Reserve System** under ECONOMY, CURRENCY) linking Federal Reserve Offices, the Board, depository institutions, the Treasury and other government agencies. Used for transferring the reserve account balances of depository institutions and government securities.

FIBOR

Frankfurt Interbank Offered Rates. These are three and six-month reference rates used as the basis for loan contracts, swaps, mark floating rate notes etc. They are calculated daily by Privat-Diskont AG, which takes the rates from 12 banks, discards the highest and the lowest, and averages the remaining 10 with a rounding to the nearest five basis points.

Fiduciary Deposits Funds held and managed strictly at a bank's or other agent's discretion but registered to the customer's account.

Fine Rate Low rate of interest on a loan. Lowest acceptable rates with narrow bid and offer rates.

Firm Offer A buy of sell order for securities that can be completed without further confirmation during a given time period.

Fiscal Agent In the Eurobond market a bank which is appointed agent for an issue, including acting as principal paying agent.

Fixed Dates Fixed or standard periods for trading Eurocurrency deposits, which range from one month to a year. See **Eurocurrency**.

Fixed Deposit Deposit repayable on a set future date with a fixed interest for the whole period.

Fixed Rate Loan Loan for a fixed period of time with a fixed interest rate for the life of a loan.

Flat Income Bond A bond traded in the USA where the price includes consideration for all unpaid accruals of interest.

Floating Charge Charge or assignment on a company's total assets as collateral for a loan.

Floating Debt Short term debt, specifically short term government debt. Also called unfunded debt.

Floating Price Rate Prime rate movements under various automatic formulae. See **Prime Rate**.

Floating Rate Bond Bond with a variable interest rate.

Floating Rate CD (FRCD) Certificate of deposit with a variable interest rate, normally linked to the London interbank money market rate. See **Certificate Of Deposit**.

Floating Rate Note (FRN) Debt security with a maturity of five to seven years. The interest rate is adjusted to money market conditions usually every six months (some are three months) with a minimum rate normally guaranteed.

Foreign Bond Issue Bond issue for a foreign borrower/guarantor underwritten by a bank or bank syndicate in one particular country, denominated in the currency of that country, placed and traded mainly within that country.

Foreign Credit Insurance Association (FCIA) US corporation owned by insurance companies providing export credit insurance.

Forward Rate Agreement (FRA) As protection against future movements in interest rates, two parties agree to a rate for a specified period form a specified future settlement date based on an agreed principal amount. No commitment is made by either party to lend or borrow the principal amount. Their exposure is only the interest difference between the agreed and actual rates at settlement time.

Front End Fees Fees paid when a loan is arranged, such as management fees.

Front End Loading Charges or fees which are greater at the start of a loan or investment contract than in its later stages.

Funded Debt Long term indebtedness of a corporation or a government resulting from the conversion of short term debt. In the UK refers to undated government stock provided an income yield whose principal the government need only repay when it wishes to do so.

Funding Process of converting short term fixed interest debt to long term fixed interest debt.

Fungible Securities Identical securities which are kept in a clearing system, where the bookkeeping is such that no specific bonds are assigned to customer accounts by their serial numbers. Only the aggregate number of identical bonds in the system and the total amount of customer holdings are controlled.

General Arrangement To Borrow (GAB) Arrangement set up in 1962 involving the members of the Group of 10 and Switzerland (then not a G-10 member) under which the countries concerned agreed to provide special credits to the IMF in their own currencies for G-10 member countries. The GAB needs the collective agreement of its members to be activated. The credits are separate from the IMF's normal resources and are only for use by a GAB member facing currency or payments difficulties.

General Mortgage Bond US securities term for a bond secured by a blanket mortgage on a corporation's property.

General Obligation Bond US tax exempt issue of a state or local government which is secured by the issuer's full faith, credit and taxing powers.

Gensaki Market
Market operated by Japanese securities houses which sell their own bonds in repurchase agreements or intermediate for others. Market rules call for maturities of less than one year, with one to three months as the most common. Sellers tap the market when they are temporarily short of funds, hoping to raise funds to invest in more attractive short term financial instruments or to benefit from arbitrage between short term securities and outright sales of bonds. Buyers use the market to manage short term funds, or for arbitrage.

Gilts
UK government stock, which carries virtually no default risk. The term is derived from the gold (now green) edge on the original stock certificates. Sometimes used to include nationalised or municipal securities, which do not strictly fall into the same category.

Give Up
Loss in yield from the sale of securities at one yield and the purchase of a similar amount of other securities with a lower yield.

Glass Steagall
US law of 1933 prohibiting commercial banks from underwriting or dealing in securities except for general obligation bonds and in selected special purpose municipal revenue bonds and US government debts. Banks challenged the act in the 1980s by offering money market funds, discount brokerage services, commercial paper and other investment services.

Go Around
Calls by the Federal Reserve, while conducting open market operations, to primary dealers in US government securities. By thus going around it informs whether it wants to purchase or sell securities, (i.e. do repurchase or reverses) and then seeks bids or offers.

Government Broker
Formerly, a stockbroker appointed to act as the UK government's agent in the British government bond market. These duties have now been taken over by the Bank of England.

Government National Mortgage Association (GNMA)
Or Ginnie Mae. Set up in the USA in 1968 to take over some of the functions of the Federal National Mortgage Association. Securities issued by the GNMA are backed by pools of mortgages. They bear a US government guarantee and are traded in an active secondary market. See **Federal National Mortgage Association (FNMA)**.

Grace Period
Length of time during which repayments of loan principal are excused. Occurs at the start of the loan period, often in connection with soft loans to developing countries, where the terms and conditions are mild.

Grey Market
Unofficial market, not subject to offical controls, when a new

security is traded before its formal offering on an "if, as and when issued" basis.

Gross Spread Difference between the price received by an issuer for its securities and the price paid by investors for the same securities. The spread equals the selling concession, together with the management and underwriting fees.

Gross Yield to Redemption Yield on a security if held to redemption, including an estimated annual capital gain, but excluding income or capital gains tax.

Guaranteed Bond US market term for a bond where the interest, principal or both are guaranteed by a person or corporation other than the issuer.

Haircut Finance Loan against collateral in the USA for less than the full value of the collateral, i.e. the loan is trimmed down.

Half Life Period before half the principal of a bond issue is redeemed.

HIBOR Hong Kong Interbank Offered Rate.

Hot Treasury Bills UK expression for Treasury bills on the day they are issued with their full term to run.

Hypothecation In the USA pledging securities as collateral, i.e. to secure the debit balance on a margin account. See entry under SHIPPING.

Income Bonds (a) In the UK fixed interest bonds provided by insurance companies; an immediate annuity. (b) In the USA bonds whose principal is guaranteed but on which interest payments are made only if earned and approved by the corporation's directors.

Income Yield In the UK the return over the next year in interest payments on a security.

Inconvertible Funds, currency or securities which cannot be freely converted into cash or other currency.

Industrial Revenue Bonds Bonds issued by US municipalities and used to sponsor industrial development. Some types are tax free.

Ineligible Bills Bills which are not eligible for rediscount e.g. at the Bank of England or other central bank.

Instalment Credit Method of buying goods by paying the cost price plus a charge for credit by instalments. The purchase remains the property of the seller until the last instalment is paid, thus acting as a security for the debt. In the UK it is known as hire purchase.

Instrument   Any type of financial debt paper.

In Syndication   A new bond issue still subject to price and trading restrictions imposed by (and on) the syndicate. Also refers to the period when a bank is trying to bring others into the deal.

Interbank   Market between banks for foreign exchange, Eurodeposits or domestic funds.

Interest Arbitrage   Switching funds between different interest-bearing instruments or countries to profit from higher interest rates.

Interest Capitalisation   When creditors agree to add the interest owed by a debtor to the principal for settlement at maturity. This gives the borrower breathing space to implement programmes to generate the funds needed to repay his loan.

Interest Cover   Ability of a borrower to pay the interest payments due on a borrowing from currently available financial resources.

Interest Periods   Different interest rates and periods under a rollover credit which may be drawn down at different times.

Interest Rate   Charge, often annual, paid by a borrower to a lender over a period of time. It is intended to compensate a lender for the sacrifice of losing immediate use of money and for the inflationary erosion of its buying power over the life of the loan and for the the risk involved in lending the money. Interest rates are sensitively responsive to the supply and demand factors of credit and to inflationary expectations.

Interest Rate Swap   The transfer between two counterparties of interest rate obligations, one of which has an interest rate fixed to maturity, while the other floats in accordance with changes in some benchmark such as Libor, US prime rate etc.

Interim Committee   Ministerial group in the International Monetary Fund that deals with proposals to reform the international monetary system. Its membership mirrors that of the IMF Board. Seven members are appointed by the USA, Britain, France, West Germany, Japan, China and Saudi Arabia. The other 15 are elected by groups of countries usually in regional associations.

International Banking Facilities   See entry under EQUITIES.

International Debt Issue   Debt issue underwritten and sold outside the country of the borrower/guarantor. It may be a foreign bond or a Eurobond.

International Development Association (IDA)
The World Bank's soft loan affiliate that lends on easy, concessionary terms to the poorest developing countries for specific development projects.

International Finance Corporation (IFC)
World Bank affiliate, whose main function is to help private enterprises in developing countries, mobilising domestic and foreign capital, including its own, for this purpose.

International Monetary Fund (IMF)
A specialised agency of the UN which provides funds to member countries under certain conditions of need and commitments of policy. The funds are usually for short-term purposes, especially balance of payments. The fund was established by the Bretton Woods Agreement on a system of differential quota subscriptions representing drawing rights and voting powers. See **Quota** and **Gold Tranche** under ECONOMY, CURRENCY, also **Interim Committee, Extended Fund Facility, Compensatory Financing, Standby Credit, Special Drawing Right** and **Conditionality**.

Investment Bank
US securities firm acting as an underwriter for new issues of bonds or stocks and as part of a syndicate redistributes the issue to investors. Also carries out other functions similar to a British merchant bank.

Invitation
Telex sent by a lead manager to prospective participants in a primary market issue especially the Euromarket. It sets out conditions and asks whether they wish to participate.

Irrevocable Credit
Credit granted by a bank which cannot be revoked provided all the conditions are fulfilled.

Issue Date
Date from which accrued interest on a security is calculated.

Issue Price
Price at which securities are sold on issue. This is at face value or par, at a discount or at a premium. Occasionally an issue may be partly paid meaning that the price at launch is met by instalments. For new bonds it is the gross price (before allowances or commissions) expressed as a percentage of principal amount.

Junior Bonds
In the USA bonds ranking lower in preference than other bonds.

Junk Bonds
High yield high risk debt instruments rated in the lower categories of credit-worthiness (below BAA by Moody's and BBB by Standard and Poor's). Often used to fund takeovers and leveraged buyouts, but also used by small and growing companies with no credit track record.

Kampo
Japan's Post Office Insurance Fund—One of the world's biggest investors. See **Yucho**.

Kassenobligation Medium term note issued via auction by the West German Federal government or state-owned entities such as the railway and postal authorities.

Kicker An added feature of a debt obligation, usually designed to enhance marketability by offering the prospect of equity participation.

Latin American Capital Markets Institute (LACPI) Based in Caracas, it co-ordinates information on regional capital market development.

Lead Manager Manager who leads a securities issue, e.g. Euroissue, and who is normally responsible for the contact with the borrower, organisation of the issue and preparation of the contracts and prospectus. He is also primarily responsible for putting together the issue syndicate (co-managers, underwriters), the selling group and for the placement of the issue. As a rule, the lead manager makes the largest commitment to take up and place bonds in the event of undersubscription. Also known as Lead Underwriter.

Lending Margins Fixed spread which borrowers agree to pay above an agreed base of interest; adjusted, usually every six months, reflecting changes in **LIBOR**.

Life Period of time or term from a security's issue date to its maturity.

Loan Stock Long term interest bearing stock issued by a company, often as a debenture.

Local Authorities British municipal governing bodies whose deposits and loans comprise an important secondary money market in London.

Lombard Rate The interest rate charged against collateral on Lombard credits, i.e. credits from the West German central bank (Bundesbank) to banks. For example, the Bundesbank accepts rediscountable trade bills and public authority bonds as collateral for its Lombard credits, which can run for up to three months. The bank regards Lombard as an emergency funding facility, not as a regular source of funds for the banks. Normally the rate is at least one percentage point above the West German discount rate.

London Interbank Offered Rate (LIBOR) The rate for Eurodollar funds, usually three or six months, although it can range from overnight to five years. Different banks may quote differing (lending) LIBOR rates simply because they use different source banks. The rate which a bank is willing to pay for such funds is the London Interbank Bid Rate (LIBID). The average of the LIBOR and LIBID rates is known as LIMEAN.

Long Term Capital Account	Balance of payments term to distinguish investment and government expenditure and receipts abroad from short term capital or hot money flows. Together with the current account it forms the basic balance of payments.
Longs	British government stocks with maturities exceeding 15 years. Elsewhere the definition starts around 10 years. Since such bonds commit investors' money for a long time, they normally pay a higher yield than short term bonds of the same quality. As interest rates rise, the prices of long bonds usually fall more sharply than the prices of shorter-term bonds. When interest rates fall, the prices of "longs" rise faster, since investors are ready to pay more for a bond that guarantees a high rate for a long time. See **Bond**.
LUXIBOR	Luxembourg Interbank Offered Rate.
Management Fee	A charge by banks for managing a securities issue or credit, especially on the Euromarkets.
Management Group	Group of financial institutions which co-ordinate closely with the lead manager in the distribution and pricing of an issue.
Mandatory Redemption	Feature of certain security or debt issues, involving the obligatory redemption by the issuer of part of the issue before full maturity through the operation of a sinking fund.
Mandate	Borrower's authorisation to proceed with a loan or bond issue on terms agreed with the loan manager.
Margin Requirements	Incremental reserve obligations on credit instrument.
Matched Book	A situation where the maturity dates for a bank's or trader's liabilities match those of his assets.
Matched Sale-Purchase Agreement	Outright sale of a security by the US Federal Reserve for immediate delivery to a dealer or a foreign central bank, with an agreement to buy back the security on a specific date, usually seven days, at the same price. Such agreements enable the Federal Reserve to withdraw reserves on a temporary basis from the banking system.
Maturity	See **Life**.
Maturity Date	Final redemption date for a bond/loan.
Mediums	British governments stocks with a life of between five and 15 years. In some markets "mediums" can start at two years.
Middle Price	The arithmetical mean of the bid price and offered price.

Mini-Max

A floating rate note which employs a minimum and a maximum coupon so that the interest payable only floats within a stated band.

Minimum Lending Rate (MLR)

The minimum rate at which the Bank of England used to lend to the discount market. From August 20 1981, kept in reserve to be used only in exceptional circumstances when strong guidance is needed to change the direction of the interest rates.

Money Market

Series of homogeneous national credit and deposit markets involving short term securities and operated by the central bank, the commercial banks and financial institutions.

Moody's

Moody's Investors Service of the USA operates a bond rating service for corporate, municipal and foreign country debt, ranking the debt from AAA to C. It is similar to Standard and Poor's, whose ratings run from AAA to D.

Moratorium

A situation when a borrower makes a formal statement that he is unable to meet all or part of his debts. It is usually a holding action designed to lead to renegotiation of outstanding debt repayments. Not to be confused with default. See **Repayment**.

Multicurrency Issue

A loan or bond involving several currencies. A bond issue may be made in a specific currency but repayable in several. A rollover credit may be available in different currencies to suit the borrower.

Multiple-Option Facility (MOF)

Usually has a note issuance facility (nif) but also the option to use other facilities (often in other currencies) up to the maximum size of the facility. Options could be a revolving credit, a swingline facility, a Euro-commercial paper programme and a medium term note facility. The facility could involve all the above or just some and each option would have its own terms and conditions.

Multiplier Formula

A method allowing an investor to take interest payments in the form of new bonds instead of cash.

Municipal Bond

Bonds issued by a state or local government and their agencies, especially in the USA. In most cases the interest is exempt from US federal taxation. However, the Tax Reform Act of 1986 put a ceiling on the amount of tax-free municipal debt that can be issued in the United State. Interest on debt sold after the cap is reached is taxable.

Naked Warrant

A warrant offered on its own instead of attached to an original bond. See **Covered Warrant** and **Warrant**.

National Debt

Total indebtedness of a national government as a result of

cumulative net budget deficits. Normally financed by the sale of different categories of government securities and debt instruments.

Negative Pledge

An undertaking by a borrower not to raise new loans giving new creditors preferential terms over existing creditors. Can also apply to the renegotiation of exisiting loans.

Negotiable CDs

See **Certificate Of Deposit**.

Net Borrowed Reserves

Margin by which borrowing from the US Federal Reserve banks outweighs excess reserves.

New Money

In a refunding operation, the amount by which the nominal value of the securities is greater than that of the maturing securities. Thus, the borrower takes in additional cash beyond the amount being repaid.

Newly Industrialising Economy (NIE)

No longer poor but not yet rich. Definitions vary but many include Brazil, Hong Kong, South Korea, Taiwan, Singapore and Greece as NIEs. The June 1988 World Economic Summit in Toronto opted to replace the term **Newly Industrialising Country (NIC)** with NIE.

Nominal Yield

Face yield of a bond identical to the interest coupon.

Non-Peformance Loan

See entry under EQUITIES.

Note

In the USA one of a range of debt securities. US Treasury notes refer to coupon securities with a maturity of one to 10 years, while municipal notes are short term promissory notes.

Note Issuance Facility (NIF)

Basically a loan with a medium-term life under which a borrower can issue notes, usually with maturities of three, six, nine and 12 months. Usually it is denominated in US dollars, but can have a multi-currency option which allows the borrower to issue notes in other currencies.

It is usually underwritten by a group of banks which guarantee the availability of funds either by buying any unsold notes at each roll-over date, or by providing a standby credit. Banks would issue certificates of deposit, non-banks promissory notes.

Obligation Bond

Type of US mortgage bond in which the face value is greater than the value of the underlying property.

Odd Lot

Any block of securities bid for or offered which is smaller than the standard lot size for the type of security.

Offering Circular

Document which describes the terms of a securities issue

and gives full financial and other information on the borrower. Also known as a prospectus.

Open Market Central bank sale or purchase of securities intended to influence the volume of money and credit in the economy. Chiefly involves short term government securities but also medium and long term issues. Purchases inject reserves into the system, thus expanding credit, while sales have the opposite effect.

Original Maturity Time to maturity of a security at the date on which it was issued.

Over-Allocation Situation where lead managers of bond issues allocate to the selling group a larger sum of bonds than is actually planned for the issue.

Overnight Repo An overnight Repurchase Agreement, whereby securities dealers and banks finance their inventories of Treasury bills, notes and bonds. They sell securities to an investor with a temporary surplus of cash, agreeing to buy them back the next day. See **Repurchase Agreement**.

Paper General term for securities, commercial paper, money market instruments etc.

Par Nominal or face value of a security, not its market price. It has more significance with bonds, indicating maturity risk, than it has with common stock. Par (face) value is used to describe the value of a bond in terms of what the company will repay when the loan matures.

Paragraph 17 Section of the West German central bank's law which allows the Bundesbank to inject government funds into the money market when liquidity is tight. The Bundesbank instructs government-owned banks to offer surplus government funds to the market.

Paris Club See entry under ECONOMY, CURRENCY.

Participation Fee Fee charged by a bank for taking part in providing a loan, e.g. in the Euromarket.

Paydown Amount by which, in a US Treasury refunding, the par value of maturing securities is greater than that of those being sold.

Paying Agent Bank of a bond issuer where principal and interest are payable.

Peformance Bond Instrument aimed at ensuring a service or contract is completed correctly. If this is not the case, then the bank issuing or guaranteeing the bond will be required to make a compensatory payment.

Perpetual Bond Bond that has no maturity date, is not redeemable and pays a steady stream of interest indefinitely.

Pfandbrief A West German mortgage bond issued by mortgage banks and secured by their mortgage lendings. Issued and traded on the domestic bond market, the Pfandbrief normally yields more than bonds issued by public authorities.

Placing Power Ability of a financial institution to place newly-issued securities with investors.

Plus Accrued Interest Applied to the price of bonds with interest accruing from the date of the last payment. A seller is therefore entitled to receive the interest, as calculated from the last interest date to the business day following the day on which the sale is made, from the buyer.

Praecipuum A bonus fee taken by the lead manager of a Eurobond. It is deducted from the management and underwriting fee.

Preferential Debts If a company is being wound up debts are classified as secured and unsecured. In both cases certain creditors have a preference over the others.

Prepayment Payment of principal made before the scheduled payment date.

Preshipment Finance Covers an exporter's costs before shipment of goods

Primary Market Market for the placing of new securities such as international, domestic and foreign bond issues and stock with investors by the group organised to handle the issue. The sale proceeds go to the issue and not to other investors. Any subsequent resale or purchase is handled on the secondary market.

Prime Rate Theoretically lowest loan interest rate charged by US banks to their best-rated corporate customers.

Principal The face amount of a security, exclusive of any premium or interest.

Prior Charges Charges on debentures, loan stock, notes etc, which rank ahead of share capital. The service of interest on such charges is a cost of running the company which must be met before any dividend is paid, and in the event of default on the conditions of the issue the repayment of such indebtedness is a charge ranking before the share capital.

Private Placement

New issue, in the form of stock or debt which has essentially been placed with a selected group, e.g. institutional investors, rather than offered to the market by an underwriting syndicate. In the USA these offerings are not subject to SEC registration requirements.

Promissory Note

Written promise to pay, used as an instrument of commodity futures trading and of direct company borrowing in the form of commercial paper. Some such instruments are negotiable. See **Schuldschein**.

Public Sector Borrowing Requirement (PSBR)

Difference in the UK between the government's expenditure and revenue. It includes local authority expenditures.

Purchase Fund

Undertaking by a borrower to buy back a certain amount of an issue within a given period if the market price of the bonds remains below a specified level, usually par.

RANs

Revenue Anticipation Notes. Short-term debt issued by US states and municipalties.

Rating

Credit-worthiness of a specific security issue or a particular borrower as evaluated by a rating agency, e.g. in the USA graded from "triple A" downwards.

Reallowances

Restrictions on the discount at which members of the Swiss "Big Bank" bond issuing syndicate are allowed to resell bonds which they have been allocated. See **"Big Bank" Syndicate**.

Redemption

Exchange of one class of securities for another or for cash by the issuer, usually at maturity.

Redemption Price

The price at which bonds may be redeemed, or called, at the issuer's option, prior to maturity.

Redemption Yield

Current yield increased or diminished to take account of the capital gain or loss on redemption.

Rediscount

Purchase before maturity by a central bank of a government obligation or other financial instrument already discounted in the money market.

Reference Bank(s)

Bank or group of banks whose interbank lending rates are used as a reference for determining the interest rate on a Floating Rate instrument.

Refinancing

(a) In banking, extending the maturity date, or increasing the amount of existing debt, or both (b) In bonds, retiring existing debt by issuing new securities to reduce the interest rate, or extend the maturity date, or both. See **Refunding** and **Repayment**.

Refunding

Rollover of (government) debt by replacing one issue by another, the maturity of which is deferred to a later date, typically by offering a straight exchange. Also the replacement of an issue by another bearing a lesser interest charge, thereby reducing the cost of servicing the debt. The latter is sometimes called refinancing.

Regulation A

(a) A Securities and Exchange Commission provision in the USA for the simplified registration of small issues of securities (b) US Federal Reserve Board statement of the means and conditions under which Federal Reserve banks make loans to member and other banks at what is called the discount window.

Regulation G

Federal Reserve Board rule regulating lenders other than commercial banks, brokers or dealers who, in the ordinary course of business, extend credit to individuals to buy or carry securities.

Regulation M

Since April 1981, this gives the Federal Reserve Board the power to regulate consumer leasing.

Regulation Q

US Federal Reserve power to impose interest rate ceilings on certificates of deposits and all time deposits, which ended in March 1986. But a ban on paying interest on demand deposits remains.

Regulation T

US Federal Reserve regulation limiting the amount of credit which can be advanced by brokers and dealers to customers to buy securities, or for margin requirements.

Regulation U

US Federal Reserve regulation governing the quantity of credit a bank can provide to its clients seeking to buy securities.

Rente

Undated French government bond.

Repayment

When a borrower runs into difficulty repaying his loans, the following options—on an ascending scale—occur:

(a) *Refinancing.* Here the borrower seeks to pay off one loan with proceeds of another from the same or another lender.

(b) *Restructuring.* The borrower arranges to replace debt of one maturity with debt of another (usually longer) maturity, and possibly with a different type of debt (e.g. issues securities to pay off a bank debt).

(c) *Rescheduling.* Here the borrower delays the moment when the principal of an existing debt is repaid. Interest should continue to flow and the banker may exact a fee and a higher margin in return for the debt extension.

(d) *Default.* This term can mean anything from failure to make an interest payment up to intent never to repay a debt at all.

(e) *Moratorium.* Here the borrower declares that he needs a certain time to sort out his affairs and that during this time he will make no repayments of principal due.

(f) *Repudiation.* The borrower declares outright his intention not to repay or service existing debt.

See **Refinancing, Rescheduling, Moratorium** and **Default**.

Repurchase Agreement (REPO)

Usually involves US Treasury or Federal agency securities. Generally transacted in denominations of five million dollars or more, these instruments are basically loan arrangements by which a holder sells the securities at a specified price under commitments to repurchase the same or similar securities at a later date. They are considered collateral for the transaction. Dealers in the New York money market use these arrangements to finance their positions. The Federal Reserve utilises such agreements to increase and withdraw bank reserves. See **Reverse Repurchase Agreement**.

In West Germany, repos usually run for about one month and are the central bank's main instrument for steering the money market and short term interest rates.

Rescheduling

Renegotiation of terms and conditions of existing borrowings, with the objective of obtaining more favourable terms. See **Repayment**.

Reserve Requirement

Percentage of deposits that by law depository institutions (e.g. banks) must set aside in their vaults or with the central bank.

Restructuring

See **Repayment**.

Retractable

Eurobond securities giving an investor the option of early redemption a set number of years before the final maturity. If this option is not exercised, the securities will not be repaid until the later maturity.

Reverse Repurchase Agreement

Repurchase agreement initiated by a lender of funds. For the US Federal Reserve a means of temporarily draining reserves through the sale of securities which are later bought back. See **Repurchase Agreement**.

Revocable Credit

Credit given under a bill of exchange revocable at any time without notice.

Revolving Credit

Line of credit against which funds may be borrowed at any time, with regular scheduled repayments of a predetermined minimum amount.

Revolving Underwriting Facilty (RUF)

Basically a note issuance facility (NIF), but underwriters are committed to providing funds. Can also be a transferable revolving underwriting facility (TRUF), which means a bank can sell its share of the facility to another bank. See **Note Issuance Facility**.

Rollover

Extension of maturity debt by issuing fresh bonds, usually for exchange. Banks often use the term when they allow a borrower to delay making a principal payment on a loan. Or, a country having difficulty in meeting its debt payments may be granted a rollover by its creditors.

Round Tripping

In the UK a situation where a company may decide to borrow from its bank using an existing line of short term credit (overdraft) and then deposit those funds in the short term money market for short term gain. The situation arises when short term money markets rates are higher than those obtaining on an overdraft facility and a profit can be made from the interest rate differential.

Running Yield

See **Current Yield**.

Running The Books

The function of a lead manager in organising all aspects of a new securities issue.

Samurai Bond

Bond issued in Japan by a foreign borrower, denominated in yen, which can be bought by non-residents of Japan.

Savings And Loan Association (S And L)

US national or state chartered institution holding savings deposits and primarily making funds available to the housing industry through home mortgages.

Schatzwechsel

West German Treasury bill. A constant offer to sell three-day such bills is maintained by the central bank to soak up excess liquidity in the money market, if interest rates fall sharply. The rate on Schatzwechsel bills is normally higher than the official discount rate but below the rate currently allocated to repurchase agreements.

Schuldschein

Schuldschein loans are private agreements in West Germany, where a borrower draws up an agreement with a large investor, usually a bank, which makes the loan. With the borrower's permission the bank can resell the loan to another investor or divide it among several of them. The loans are traded on an interbank market.

Seasoned Securities

Bonds actively traded in the secondary market and freely available. They generally trade without restrictions on when investors can buy them.

Secondary Market

Telephone/telex and over the counter market for the sale and purchase of international and foreign bonds or domestic securities after initial issue on primary markets. The proceeds of the sale are received by an investor and not by the corporation or governmental unit underlying the transaction. See **Primary Market**.

Secured Loans And Notes

Loans in support of which some specific property belonging to the debtor is charged.

Securities And Exchange Commission

Official US body established by the Securities Exchange Act of 1934. Charged with regulatory oversight and administering rules associated with all parts of the securities industry.

Securitisation

The repackaging of securities such as mortgages, bank loans etc. into other securities, usually bonds. Also often simply refers to the borrower selling bonds, bills, notes etc. to investors rather than raising a loan from a bank.

Sell Down

Portion of a new security offered to likely participants outside the underwriting syndicate.

Selling Concession

Discount at which securities in a new issue offering are allocated to members of a selling group by the underwriters.

Selling Group Members

Those invited by a lead manager to place a securities issue. The group consists of all syndicate members plus other banks and securities dealers. Members report their subscription result to the lead manager and thereupon receive an allotment depending on their results and on their position and reputation as placers. They are allocated a set time, the selling period. Unlike syndicate members, they assume none of the risk of underwriting the securities.

Senior Issue

Fixed income securities, the holders of which have priority over the claims of creditors.

Serial Bonds

Bonds with a series of staggered maturities, more frequently US municipal bonds than corporate.

Shogun Bond

Bond not denominated in yen but issued in Japan by foreign concerns.

Short Bill

Bill of exchange payable on demand or within a very short time.

Short Dates

Standard Eurodeposit periods from overnight up to three weeks.

Short Term Capital Account

Balance of payments account depicting movements in short term funds.

SIAC

Securities Industries Automation Corporation. An independent organisation established by the New York and

American Stock Exchange as a jointly owned subsidiary to provide automated data processing, clearing and communications services.

SIBOR Singapore Interbank Offered Rate.

Sinking Fund Regular, mandatory prepayments by a borrower, regardless of price movements in the secondary bond market, to redeem a certain amount of an issue through payments to a special account, thus reducing the principal amount due at maturity.

Soft Loan Loan or credit granted at below market rates and often over a longer period than normal, especially to developing countries.

Sovereign Risk Risk that a foreign government will default on its loan or fail to honour other business commitments because of a change in national policy. This risk results in banks normally observing limits on the amount of lending they will make to any single government or organisation whose borrowing is guaranteed by that government. Such a sovereign risk is, however, more acceptable than one incurred on a loan not subject to government guarantee.

Special Deposits Form of reserve requirement operated by a central bank, e.g. the Bank of England under which banks may be required to maintain a percentage of their deposits at the central bank.

Special Drawing Right (SDR) See entry under ECONOMY, CURRENCY.

Split Spread Normally applies to a Eurocredit with different spreads over **LIBOR** for different periods of the credit.

Spread For new securities the flotation cost or the amount by which the offering price exceeds the proceeds received by the issuer. See entry under COMMODITIES.

Stabilisation The process enabling issue managers to stabilise the price of new issues in the secondary market. By taking long or short positions, the managers aim to influence the market price through purchases or sales.

Standard & Poor's Corporation US firm which operates a bond rating service, ranking the debt from AAA to D. See **Moody's**.

Standby Credit Arrangement with a lender (either a group of banks, or the IMF in the case of a member country) that a fixed amount of credit will be available for drawing during a given period, if required.

Straight Bond Bond, often a Eurobond, which is not convertible into equity. Some straights may be redeemed early through a purchase or sinking fund.

Stripped Securities In the USA, zero coupon notes and bonds created by securities firms to give investors participation in interest or principal payments on underlying US Treasury or municipal securities. The buyer purchases these "strips" at a discount and receives only a single payment at maturity. The difference between the purchase price and the maturity value provides the investor's return.

Student Loan Marketing Association (SLMA) Known as Sallie Mae. A publicly traded US stock corporation which guarantees student loans traded on the secondary market.

Subordinated Debt Debt with status junior to other current outstanding debt of the same issuer. In the event of bankruptcy, senior creditors are paid off first.

Sushi Straight Eurocurrency bond issued by Japanese borrowers and targeted at Japanese investors.

Syndicate Group of investment banks or financial institutions which guarantee to buy (underwrite) on a wholesale basis a new securities issue from the issue and offer it for resale to investors. A group of banks which join together to raise medium term finance for governments, financial institutions or other entities.

Tankoku Japanese government paper with maturities of six months. Introduced in February 1986 as a way of helping to smooth out refunding of huge amounts of previously issued 10-year government bonds.

Tap Stock British government bond of short, medium, or long term maturity, issued at a stated price and used to control the gilts market. Supplies to the market may be turned on or off, hence the term tap. In general, a tap issue means a type of financing where only a portion of the full principal amount is initially issued; the rest follows later, depending upon market conditions or the need of the issuer.

Taux Annuel Monetaire (TAM) Interest rate for certain French floating rate domestic bond issues. Based on annualised money market rates.

Taux Moyen Des Emprunts d'Etat (TME) Interest rate for some floating rate French domestic bonds. Based on the average yield of medium and long term state issues.

Tax Anticipation Bill (TAB)
Formerly a short term money instrument sold by the US Treasury to smooth the inflow of corporate tax payments. Known in the UK as a tax reserve certificate.

Term Bond
Issue with all bonds maturing on the same day.

Term Fed Funds
US Federal funds sold for longer than the usual overnight.

Term Loan
Loan for fixed period usually more than one year.

Third Window
Alternative low interest source of lending to developing nations by the World Bank.

Tied Loan
Country to country loan requiring the recipient state to purchase goods or services from the donor.

Time Deposit
Bank deposit of fixed maturity.

Tokkin
Special money trust accounts operated by Japanese trust banks for institutional investors.

Tombstone
Advertisment for a stock, bond or syndicated credit issue not including the issue price, appearing in newspapers and magazines as a matter of record. It usually describes the site and type of issue, and the composition of the syndicate.

Topping Up
In finance, a clause whereby a borrower records his agreement to deposit further security if the lender asks for it.

Trading Paper
Certificates of deposit expected to be traded by purchasers on Euromarkets.

Tranche
An agreed instalment of a credit or loan, which may be drawn down as required. Also refers to a country's drawings from the IMF which are made in tranches.

Treasury Bill
Short term government bearer security (not more than one year, usually three to six months) sold on a regular basis and commanding a dominating position on money markets. It is sold at a discount from par being short term. The purchase and sale of such bills, i.e. through open market operations, form a key part of monetary policy. In the US auctions of 91-day and 182-day bills take place weekly, and their yields are watched closely for clues to interest rate trends.

Treasury Bonds
Long term debt of 10 years or more.

Treasury Notes
One to 10 year US Treasury security.

Treasury Stock
See entry under EQUITIES.

Underwriter One who undertakes to place a certain amount of a bond, stock or share offering by purchasing them for resale to investors. The offering may be purchased outright through a syndicate.

Unsecured Loans And Notes Securities issued by a company without specifically charging all or any of the assets.

Value Date See entry under GENERAL MARKET TERMS.

Vanilla Bond A straight fixed rate bond issue which has the terms and conditions usually accepted as being conventional to a particular securities market.

Variable Rate Financial instrument of security bearing a variable interest rate. Can be applied to certificates of deposit issue for a normal minimum period of 360 days with the interest rate set at a specified spread over the current rate of 90-day CDs. Such CDs are adjusted every 90 days.

Variable Redemption Bond Bond in which the amount repaid is tied to some variable, i.e. yen/dollar exchange rate, performance of the US Treasury 30-year bond, a stock exchange index or the gold price. Such bonds are often issued in bull and bear portions or tranches, where the bull redemption price rises and falls with the variable, while the bear redemption price moves in the opposite direction. Also known as "Bull and Bear" bonds, or "Heaven and Hell" bonds.

Warrant Certificate, often attached to a bond or security, giving the holder limited or perpetual rights to buy securities or other assets at a set price or to subscribe to future bond issues by the same issuer. Warrantable bonds are those acquired through the exercise of the certificate. See **Covered Warrant** and **Naked Warrant**.

Washing Purchase and sale of a security, either simultaneously or very close together, often used as a way to avoid tax. In the UK washing is not illegal, but changes in the tax law mean it is no longer advantageous for tax purposes.

When Issued (W/I) Short for "when, as and if issued". It refers to a transaction made conditionally because a security, although authorised, has not yet been formally issued. For US Treasury issues this is the period from the announcement of the issue until the time after the sale when payment has been actually received by the Treasury.

World Bank Main international agency for channelling aid funds, usually medium-term, for capital and human resource projects to developing countries. Set up under the Bretton Woods agreement of 1944 which also established the International

Monetary Fund. The bank may channel private funds and make loans from its own resources. It also raises money by selling bonds on the world market. Its official title is the International Bank for Reconstruction and Development (IBRD). See **International Development Association, International Finance Corporation**.

Yankee Bond Bond issued in the USA by a foreign borrower in US currency and registered with the Securities and Exchange Commission. No withholding tax is payable.

Yield Percentage return on an investment, usually at an annual rate.

Yield Curve A diagram showing the relationship between yields and maturities for a set of similar securities or interbank deposits. An ascending, positive or normal yield curve slope is characterised by interest rates rising as maturities lengthen. A horizontal or flat slope is characterised by similar yield levels for all maturities. A descending, negative or inverted slope is characterised by interest rates falling as maturities lengthen.

Yield To Maturity Takes into account for a bond the price discount or the premium over the fact value. It is larger than the current yield when the bond sells at a discount and smaller than the current yield when the bond sells at a premium.

Yucho Japan's Post Office Savings Fund—One of the world's biggest investors. See **Kampo**.

Z Certificates Certificates issued by the Bank of England in lieu of stock certificates to discount houses to facilitate their dealings in short dated stock. The certificates are issued as soon as a transfer of stock is lodged with the bank and can be split into smaller denominations if required. They are readily acceptable as collateral against loans.

Zero Coupon Discount basis corporate credit instrument issued with imputed interest calculated on the price paid by the buyer and the par value at which the bond will be redeemed. Typically such a bond could be issued in the amount of 200 million dollars, the price paid at redemption. It would provide the borrower with an immediate cash amount of less than the half the value. Under some jurisdictions, zero coupon securities have tax benefits for both borrowers and investors.

Zoo The acronyms of many debt instruments suggest they might be found in a banker's zoo. Examples include CATS (Certificate of Accrual on Treasury Securities), LYON (Liquid Yield Option Note), STAGS (Sterling Transferable Accruing

Securities), TIGER (Treasury Investors Growth Receipt), and ZEBRA (Zero Coupon Eurosterling Bond).

Equities

Accelerated Depreciation

Accrual of depreciation under a method that results in reporting a decreasing amount of depreciation expense each year over the life of the asset. See **Depreciation**.

Acceptance

An agreement by a shareholder to take up an offer made to him.

Accession Rate

Additional employees hired as a percentage of total employment. Also called hiring rate.

Account

(a) The principal division of the UK stock exchange calendar, normally runs for two weeks (10 working days). During this period deals are done for settlement on account day. There are 24 account periods in a year. (b) In the USA, a broker's record of a customer's transactions.

Account Day

Also called **Settlement Day** in the UK. The day on which all bargains for the account are settled. Normally the second Monday following the end of the account.

Account Trading

Practice of buying and selling the same securities within a single account period, meaning that the investor then only needs to settle with his broker the difference between his buying and selling prices, plus commission charges.

Accumulated Depreciation

Total depreciation expense accrued from the date of the purchase to the present.

Acid Test Ratio

Simple ratio of a company's liquid assets to current liabilities. Such assets include cash, marketable securities and accounts receivable.

Acquisition

Takeover of one company by another.

Acting in Concert

Investors working together to achieve the same goal, e.g. buy all the stock in a company they want to take over.

Affiliate

Two companies are called affiliates, if one owns less than a majority of the voting stock of the other, or if both are subsidiaries of a third company.

After Tax Real Rate Of Return

Net yield obtained from nominal rate of return after tax minus the inflation rate.

Allotment

Allocation of securities from a new issue. If the issue proves popular, the allotment may be made as a percentage of the amount of shares applied for. In the Eurobond and US securities markets, it refers to the allocation of securities to members of the syndicate involved in the issue.

Allotment Letter   Informs the addressee of the number of shares he has been allotted. The letter is of value and may act as a temporary or permanent certificate.

American Depositary Receipt (ADR)   Issued by US banks to facilitate trading in foreign stocks or shares. The holder is entitled to all dividends and capital gains.

Anti-Trust Laws   US Federal legislation to prevent monopolies and restraint of trade.

Application Form   Special form when applying for securities offered for sale.

Asset Stripping   Seeking a profit through buying a company cheaply, when its market price is below the value of its assets, and then selling off most of its assets.

Assets   What a company owns or is owed. Cash, investment, monies due, material and stocks are equivalent to current assets. Plant, machinery and property are fixed assets. Patents and goodwill represent intangible assets. See **Liabilities**.

Authorised Capital/Stock   Maximum amount of all classes of stocks and shares which a company is authorised to issue by its shareholders, but different from issued capital. See **Issued Capital** and **Market Capitalisation**.

Azioni Di Risparmio   A non-voting category of shares issued by Italian companies which give a marginally higher dividend than ordinary shares.

Back Up   Reverse a stock market trend.

Backdoor Listing   When a company is listed on the stock exchange after acquiring an already listed company and injecting into it new activities. This method can prove quicker and cheaper than if the originally unlisted company went through full listing procedures.

Balance Certificate   Issued to a shareholder when he has sold only part of the shares represented by a share certificate.

Balance Sheet   Summary of assets and liabilities at a given date. It is not an exact statement of financial position as the figures are a mix of fact and estimate, reflecting the position as fairly and accurately as possible. See **Assets, Liabilities**.

Balance Sheet Ratios   Extracted from the balance sheet, these provide information about a company's performance. Important ratios include the liquidity ratio, gross profit as a percentage of turnover, net profit as a percentage of gross profit, the level of credit given compared to turnover, and the rate of stock turnover. See **Liquidity Ratios**.

Bank Holding Company

US term for a company which owns or controls one or more banks. The Federal Reserve Board has responsibility for regulating and supervising such companies.

Bankruptcy

A company becomes formally bankrupt following a court ruling that it is unable to meet its debts. The ruling may be sought either by the company concerned (voluntary liquidation) or by creditors. In England an official receiver is appointed by the court to manage and eventually realise the debtors' assets on behalf of the creditors. Different procedures are followed in other countries. See **Chapter 11**.

Banque d'Affaires

French investment bank similar to a British merchant bank.

Bargain

Any stock exchange transaction. No special price is implied.

Basic Point Price

System under which delivered prices in a specific industry represent the cost at a number of production centres plus a standard freight charge for the same distance. Prices are thus standard whatever the base used.

Big Bang

Nickname for the change in UK Stock Exchange rules and practices, bringing them more into line with those of major overseas exchanges such as New York. The first rule changes, which permitted financial institutions such as banks and insurance companies to own Stock Exchange subsidiaries, came into force on March 1, 1986. These were followed on October 27, 1986, by the introduction of new electronic dealing systems, abolition of the strict segregation between (retailing) brokers and (wholesaling) jobbers, and an end to fixed commissions. See **May Day**.

Big Board

New York Stock Exchange price display.

Block Trading

Transacting large stock lots, usually in excess of 10,000 shares among institutional purchasers or sellers.

Blue Chip

Common stock of companies with proven management skills and expertise. Usually involves major companies with sound earnings and dividend records and above average share performance. Extremely well known and regarded corporations. Originally American, this term derives from the highest valued poker chip.

Blue Sky Laws

US state (not Federal) laws enacted to protect the public against securities frauds.

Bonus Issue See **Capitalisation Issue**.

Book Value (a) Value of a corporation determined by dividing the number of issued shares into a company's net assets. Also known as net asset value. (b) Value at which an asset is carried on a balance sheet. An item's book value at any time is its cost minus accumulated depreciation.

Booked Expression for the book-keeping entries connected with a given transaction being entered in a country other than where the transaction takes place. Normally done to lessen tax liability.

Bottom Line The final or real cost or result. The term derives from companies' profit and loss accounts, in which the bottom line shows the extent of the profit (or loss) after all income and expenses have been accounted for.

Breakeven Point (a) Securities term meaning price at which a transaction produces neither a profit nor a loss. (b) In finance, point at which sales equal costs.

Broker In the context of Big Bang, an "agency broker" is regarded as the traditional stockbroker acting solely as an agent and charging commission. A "broker dealer" is the new-style stockbroker who will both make a market in shares and buy from/sell to his clients. Brokers who charge lower commission rates but give no advice or research information are known as "discount brokers". See entry under GENERAL MARKET TERMS.

Building Society British institution which accepts deposits, pays interest on them and grants loans for house purchases, secured by mortgages. In the USA, Savings and Loan Association.

Buyout The purchase of at least a controlling interest in a company's stock to take over its assets and operations. See **Leveraged Buyout**.

CAC Index Paris bourse index provided by the Compagnie des Agents de Change. Calculated according to the value of 244 shares which together represent about 85 per cent of the market's capitalisation.

Call Amount due to be paid to company by the purchaser of nil paid or partly paid shares. See entry under GENERAL MARKET TERMS.

Callable Capital Unpaid-up part of a company's capital which can be called for payment to be made.

Capacity Utilisation Ratio of output compared to the full capacity of a company, industrial sector or economy. A key to the level of economic activity.

Capital Equity of a company representing net worth in the form of issued stock at book value and retained net earnings.

Capital Allowances Allowances against tax on expenditure on capital equipment used by industry or business.

Capital Base Issued capital of a company, plus reserves and retained profits. See **Issued Capital, Reserves,** and **Retained Profits**.

Capital Employed Capital used in a business. It may refer to net assets but often includes bank loans and overdrafts.

Capital Expenditure Payment for the acquisition of a long-term asset such as land, plant or machinery.

Capital Gain Increase in the value of a capital asset when it is sold or transferred compared to its initial worth. Inflation and currency movements can affect the "real" capital gain. Capital loss is the opposite, i.e. when the sale of an asset yields less than the acquisition cost.

Capital Gearing Relationship between the different types of capital used by a company. See **Gearing**.

Capital Goods Typically fixed assets such as plant or machinery used in the manufacture of other goods. Also called capital equipment.

Capital Intensive Use of relatively large amounts of capital to raise production, instead of increasing the contribution of other inputs, e.g. the labour force or raw materials.

Capital Investment Investment by a government or company in capital goods.

Capitalisation Total market value of a company's issued shares, the amount of a company's capital, as well as its composition, i.e. debt, equity.

Capitalisation Issue An issue of shares which results from a company transferring money from its reserves to its permanent capital. These new shares are then distributed to the existing holders in proportion to their existing holdings. Also known as a free, bonus or scrip issue.

Carryover Carrying over the settlement of account on the stock exchange until the next account period, by the payment of interest. See entry under COMMODITIES.

Carryover Day   UK stock exchange term for the settlement day which starts each new trading account of approximately two weeks duration.

Cartel   When businesses, organisations or countries group together and agree, often implicitly, to influence the price or supply of goods.

Cash Dividend   Cash payment to a company's shareholders, distributed from current earnings or accumulated profits and taxable as income. It is distinguished from stock dividend, which involves payment in the form of stock.

Cash Flow   Sum of pre-tax profits and depreciation allowances. See **Net Cash Flow**.

Cash Ratio   Ratio of cash and related assets to liabilities; in the case of a bank, the ratio of cash to total deposit liabilities.

Chapter 11   Under this aspect of US bankruptcy laws, a debtor, unable to pay his debts, remains in possession of his business and in control of its operations, unless a court rules otherwise. Chapter 11 gives debtors and creditors considerable flexibility in working together to reorganise the business.

Chinese Walls   Term for boundaries between departments in financial conglomerates to stop conflicts of interest—e.g. a corporate finance team should not notify an in-house market maker of a coming bid.

City Bank   Japanese term for a commercial bank. These are distinguished from rural banks, which mainly lend to and take deposits from farmers; wholesale or long-term banks, which may issue longer-term debt than other banks and relend the proceeds; and trust banks, which manage trust funds.

Clearing Bank   Member bank of a national cheque clearing system. To "clear" a cheque means to process it through the clearing system, so that the payee receives its value.

Close Company   UK term for a company controlled by five or fewer persons whether directors or otherwise. The US equivalent is the closed company.

Closed End (Investment) Company   Investment company with a fixed capital structure, with a number of fixed shares outstanding which are traded in the secondary market and cannot be redeemed or increased.

Closed Shop   A business or industry in which employees must be members of particular trade unions.

Commercial Bank Bank concentrating principally on short term industrial and commercial lending. Typically such an institution will offer a broad range of services to business and consumers, including current (checking) accounts, commercial, consumer and mortgage loans.

Commerzbank Index West Germany's Commerzbank AG publishes an index of 60 leading shares on the Düsseldorf bourse. It is calculated at mid-session, not the close. See **DAX Index, FAZ Index**.

Commission des Opérations de Bourse (COB) Official French watchdog agency for stock exchange transactions.

Common Stock US equivalent of ordinary shares. See **Ordinary Capital**.

Competitive Trader Member of the New York Stock Exchange trading in stocks for an account in which he has an interest.

Company Doctor Colloquially, a management expert or consultant engaged to diagnose the problems of an ailing company and remedy them by recommending policy changes and corporate reorganisation.

Conglomerate Corporation with widely diversified interests, normally built up by acquisition.

Consolidated Balance Sheet Shows the financial situation of a corporation and its subsidiaries.

Consolidated Tape Tape which since 1975 has reported transactions in listed securities on the NYSE, AMEX and US regional stock exchanges.

Consolidation (a) Taking of profits which have been made on speculative shares and reinvesting the proceeds in more conservative stocks. (b) Accounting method used in presenting financial statements. (c) US term for a combination or fusion of two or more companies into a new company. (d) Substitution of national currencies held in a country's exchange reserves by a new international monetary asset, e.g. Special Drawing Rights.

Consortium Group of companies formed to promote a common objective or project.

Consortium Bank Specialised bank with a group of other banks as shareholders but where no single bank holds a majority of the equity. Usually involved in large scale international financing operations via the Euromarkets.

Contango	Charge made by a stockbroker in the UK for carrying over a position from one account to another without paying for or delivering a stock. Contango Day is the last dealing day of an account, on which contangos are arranged. See entry under COMMODITIES.
Continental Depositary Receipt (CDR)	Bearer document allowing trading to take place in US, UK and Japanese registered company shares on certain European exchanges.
Contract	Agreement between two or more parties intended to be legally enforceable. See entry under COMMODITIES.
Conversion Price	See entry under LENDING.
Correspondent Bank	Bank that accepts deposits of and performs banking services for other depository institutions in centres where the others are not physically represented.
Cover	Extent to which a company's dividend and/or interest disbursement is matched or exceeded by its earnings.
CQS	Consolidated Quotation System. A US system which electronically collects and disseminates current bids and asking quotations, with size, from and to all market centres in which listed stocks are traded.
Credit Unions	Financial co-operation organisation in the USA comprising individuals with a common affiliation, e.g. employer, neighbourhood. They accept members' deposits in the form of share purchases, pay interest out of earnings while providing consumer instalment credit for their members.
Cum	(a) Latin for "with", used in abbreviations such as Cum Cap, Cum Div and Cum Rights to indicate the share buyer is entitled to participate in a forthcoming capitalisation issue, dividend or rights issue, (b) Short for "cumulative" as in Cum Pref, meaning cumulative preference share.
Cum All	Including all supplementary advantages attached to a share. Opposite is **Ex All**.
Cum Capitalisation	The share price including free shares issued to shareholders under a capitalisation issue.
Cum Coupon	The situation where the purchaser of securities is entitled to receive the next interest payment. See entry under LENDING.
Cum Rights	Shares sold which include any rights attached to them.

Cumulative

Stock or share, generally preference or preferred, the ownership of which carries an entitlement to receive dividend arrears before payment out of current profits is made on stock and ordinary shares, not carrying this entitlement.

Currency Exchange

Agreement whereby two companies in different countries agree to cover specific foreign exchange needs by matching loans in their national currencies. It does not require an exchange of currency between the two countries.

Current Assets

Corporate assets which can be realised reasonably quickly. These include stock in trade, work in progress, bank balances and marketable securities. In the USA it can be defined as cash, US government bonds, receivables, monies usually due within one year and inventories.

Current Liabilities

Counterpart of current assets, representing reasonably short term working commitments of a company. These include trade creditors, sums due to banks, taxation payable and declared dividends.

Current Liquidity Ratio

Current liabilities minus liquid (current) assets divided by profit or cash flow multiplied by 365 (days).

Current Profit

In the Japanese context, profits before tax and after deduction of production/administration/sales costs as well as of non-operating profit or loss and miscellaneous items.

Current Ratio

Balance sheet ratio of current assets over current liabilities. The difference between the two is net working capital which provides a guide to the company's level of liquidity.

Current Yield

(a) In the UK a flat or running yield (as opposed to a redemption yield). It is the annual return which an investor would secure by investing £100 at the current price in a security paying a known dividend. It is calculated by multiplying the annual dividend rate percent by the nominal value of the security and dividing by the price, the last two items being of the same denomination. It takes no account of the profit or loss, if any, on redemption, nor of the tax payable by the investors. (b) In the USA, the percentage return obtained by dividing current dollar income by the market price of the stock or bond.

Date of Record

Date on which a shareholder must officially own shares in order to be entitled to a dividend.

Dawn Raid

Term for the acquisition of shares at a price which results in the purchase of a large block of equity in a company in a short space of time. Typically, such purchases took place at the start of trading.

DAX Index Frankfurt Stock Exchange minute-by-minute blue chip index.

Daylight Exposure Limit Limits on a bank's foreign exchange business during a working day, either overall or by currency.

Dealing Within The Account Purchase and sale of shares within the same account.

Debenture See entry under LENDING.

Deed of Arrangement In the UK, arrangement made between a debtor and creditor to try to avoid bankruptcy or liquidation.

Deed Of Transfer Document authorising a company to transfer stock from one shareholder to another.

Defensive Stocks Shares with a high yield, low price/earnings ratio and modest prospects for price appreciation. Normally found in economic sectors less subject to cyclical fluctuations.

Depletion Accounting Accounting practice consisting of charges against earnings based upon the amount of an asset taken out of total reserves of the asset in a given accounting period.

Depreciation Reduction in the book value of a corporate fixed asset over the asset's economic life, or reduction in the market value of a currency.

Demerger Opposite of a merger (combining several companies into one entity). A demerger puts parts of a company into separate companies because they are expected to perform better.

Dilution Reduction in per share participation in net earnings through an increase in issued stock. In the USA fully diluted earnings per share are earnings after assuming the exercise of warrants and stock options, and the conversion of convertible bonds and preferred stock.

Direct Investment (a) Corporate investment in the producer side of a foreign economy, as distinct from portfolio investment. (b) A stake in a company or venture which brings a say in how it is run.

Discounted Cash Flow Accounting techniques for establishing the relative worth of a future investment project by discounting the expected cash flows from the project against its net present value.

Disinvestment Lowering capital investment by getting rid of capital goods (such as plant and machinery) or by failing to replace capital assets when they are used up.

Distributed Profits Profits distributed to shareholders via dividend payments.

Distribution Stock US term for part of a block of shares sold over a period of time to avoid upsetting the market price.

Dividend Cash or stock payment to shareholders, variable in the case of ordinary or common shares, fixed in the case of preferred shares. Even if a company is doing badly, it may make a payment of past earnings. In the USA the payment cannot be greater than the retained earnings account. Failure to pay a dividend is known as "passing" it. See also **Interim Dividend** and **Final Dividend**.

Dividend Cover See **Cover**.

Dividend-Right Certificate A Swiss security similar to "participation certificates", which does not confer ownership but instead gives a right to a share in a company's profits or any proceeds from its liquidation. Known as Genussschein in German, bon de jouissance in French.

Dividend Yield Current dividend as a percentage of a share's market price.

Double Taxation Application of two separate taxes or tax systems to a source of income or capital.

Dow Jones Index The Dow Jones Industrial Average (DJIA) measures the average price of 30 blue chip shares, primarily industrials on the New York Stock Exchange. Separate subindexes cover transportation and utilities.

Dual Capacity As a result of London reforms, securities firms are now able to perform the functions of both jobbers and brokers. As new broker/dealers some are called market markers, meaning that they undertake to buy and sell shares continuously under a strict code of practice. See **Big Bang**.

Dual Listing Security which is listed on more than one stock exchange.

Dual Pricing Identical product sold at different prices in different markets.

Dumping In the USA can refer to sales of large amounts of stock with little concern for its effect on prices. See entry under ECONOMY, CURRENCY.

Duopoly Market in which there are two dominant sellers of a particular item or service.

Earning Power Company's ability to earn sufficient profit to cover its own needs and those of its shareholders.

Earnings Per Share (EPS) One gauge of a company's performance arrived at by dividing the company's earnings by the number of shares on issue.

Earnings Yield — Hypothetical rate of return which an investor would obtain from 100 shares if all the company's latest annual profits were distributed, divided by the current price for 100 shares.

Effective Yield — Actual rate of return obtained by an investor who acquires and then sells a security.

Efficient Portfolio — Portfolio providing a maximum expected return for a given risk, or minimum risk for a given return.

Entitlement Issue — Similar in Australia to a rights issue, except that it cannot be traded on to someone else. The shareholder has the option to take it up or let it lapse. See **Rights**.

Entrepreneur — Someone who puts up funds for an enterprise, and thus undertakes the risk.

Equity — The risk-sharing part of a company's capital. Refers to ordinary share or common stock, as distinct from preference or loan capital. See entry under COMMODITIES.

Equity Accounting — When one firm holds less than a controlling interest in another, it can elect, in some countries, to account on its books a percentage of the profit of its associate, based on its actual state and irrespective of whether that profit percentage has been paid out in the form of dividend. For example, if company A holds 33 per cent of company B, it could claim—on paper at least—33 per cent of B's profit.

Escalator Clause — (a) Clause in a contract, typically a capital project, allowing a price increase payable to the contractor to help offset cost inflation. (b) Clause in a wage contract giving automatic pay increases when the cost of living rises beyond agreed thresholds.

Ex — Without (the opposite of "Cum"). Used to indicate that the buyer is not entitled to participate in whatever forthcoming event is specified. Abbreviated to XD for ex-dividend.

Ex All — Without all supplementary advantages attaching to a share. Opposite to **Cum All**.

Ex Cap — Ex capitalisation, excluding the rights of scrip or capitalisation issues attaching to a share. Opposite is **Cum Cap**.

Ex Div (XD) — Ex dividend, excluding the right to the current dividend on a share. Opposite is **Cum Dividend**.

Ex Factory/Mill/ Warehouse — Delivery term based on the price quoted, i.e. the buyer will pick up the goods at the factory or warehouse.

Ex Rights   Excluding the rights to an issue of shares for cash made by a company to its existing shareholders. Opposite is **Cum Rights**.

Exchange Distribution   Method of filling an order to sell a large block of stock on the floor of the New York Stock Exchange, by seeking buy orders and crossing them with the sell order.

Extra Dividend   Dividend paid in addition to the regular payment, perhaps after a particularly profitable year.

Extraordinary Items   Income or expenses outside the normal course of a company's business.

Factor Cost   The cost of producing one item, including labour and ingredients, as distinct from its market price which could be affected by indirect taxes and subsidies.

FAZ Index   An index of 100 leading shares quoted on the Frankfurt Bourse and calculated from official fixing prices by West Germany's Frankfurter Allgemeine Zeitung (FAZ) daily newspaper.

Federal Trade Commission (FTC)   A US agency administering both anti-trust and consumer protection laws.

FIFO   First in, first out. A principle of accounting by which the valuation of a company's stocks is based on the assumption that goods are used in the order of purchase; thus, those bought earlier (first), are used earlier (first). Opposite is LIFO, last in, first out.

Final Dividend   Dividend paid out by a company at the end of its financial year and authorised by shareholders at their annual general meeting. See **Interim Dividend**.

Financial Intermediaries, Managers and Broker Regulatory Association, (FIMBRA)   UK self-regulatory organisation (SRO) which regulates independent investment advisers such as insurance brokers selling equity linked life policies and other products. See **Self-Regulatory Organisation (SRO)**.

Financial Times (FT) Index   Measures the average value of 30 leading industrial and commercial shares quoted in London. Popular since 1935 as being the only index calculated hourly throughout the trading day. However, since 1984 an index of 100 leading UK shares (known as the FT-SE 100 index or Footsie) provides a minute by minute picture of how values are moving.

Financial Year Year used for accounting purposes. It may be the same as the calendar year or cover a different period. E.g. April to March. Also called Fiscal Year.

Fixed Assets Land, buildings, plant, equipment and other assets acquired for carrying on the business of a company with a life exceeding one year. Normally expressed in accounts at cost, less accumulated depreciation.

Fixed Capital Similar to Fixed Assets except purchased out of paid up capital.

Fixed Charges Operational or business expenses which are fixed and have no set relation to varying output levels.

Franked Dividend In Australia, a dividend paid out of profits subject to tax at the company tax rate.

Garage (a) To transfer assets or liabilities elsewhere, either to a different centre or different company normally with the intention of reducing tax liability. (b) One of the floor sections on the New York Stock Exchange.

Gearing Relationship between loan capital, preference capital and ordinary capital. It can be expressed in terms of either nominal value or market capitalisation value. High gearing means that prior charges and/or senior issues are large in relation to the equity or ordinary shares. Low gearing means the reverse.
   Usage is often confusing in that it can refer to financial or operational gearing. A highly-geared balance sheet is one where debt is large in relation to equity capital. Heavy operational gearing is found, for example, among airlines and hotels, where fixed costs account for a relatively high proportion of total costs. See **Leverage**.

Glamour Stock Stocks which achieve a wide following by producing steadily rising sales and earnings over a long period.

Gogo Fund High risk investment fund or unit trust intended to produce a greater than average increase in value by speculation.

Going Public When a privately-owned company decides to issue shares to the general public, often to raise money for an expanding business.

Gold Shares Shares in gold mining companies, mainly South African and Australian.

Golden Handcuffs US term often used to refer to a contract binding an executive to a company by offering substantial incentives. If the employee then leaves, he must pay back much of this "compensation".

Golden Parachute   Lavish benefits offered to a top executive, if job loss results, when his company is taken over.

Greenmail   Used notably in the USA to describe payments by the target of a takeover to a potential bidder, usually to buy back acquired shares at a premium. In return the predator agrees not to pursue the bid further.

Gross Processing Margin   Difference between the cost of raw materials and the sales revenue from finished products.

Gross Profit   Total profit before deduction of tax and expenses.

Gross Sales   Total sales at invoice value (i.e. without customer discounts etc.).

Gross Yield   Pre-tax return on a security.

Gross Yield to Redemption   See entry under LENDING.

Grossing Up   Calculating the amount of tax required, in the case of an investment subject to tax, to equal the income from an investment not subject to tax.

Growth Stock   Shares in a company which has been growing faster-than-average and which are expected to continue to do so.

Hammering   UK term for the announcement of the failure of a Stock Exchange firm. The exchange maintains a compensation fund to recompense investors, should a member firm fail to meet its obligations.

High-Tech Stock   Companies in high-technology fields such as computers, biotechnology and electronics.

Hire Purchase   Buying goods through instalment payments. See **Instalment Credit** under LENDING.

Historic Cost   Original cost of a company's assets as distinct from replacement cost.

Holding Company   Corporation or company controlling one or several companies through ownership of their stock, in most cases with voting control. Often used to bring together and supervise the interests of large corporations, or to facilitate diversification.

Hot Stock	Stock in great public demand, often a new issue, which rises quickly in price.
Imputation	In Australia, a system whereby an investor pays no tax on a dividend. The company distributes a dividend, having already paid tax on the profits from which it is distributed.
Incorporation	When a US state charter is granted to a company, allowing it to operate as a corporation with the term "incorporated" or Inc. in its legal name.
Independent Broker	Broker on the floor of the New York Stock Exchange who executes orders for other brokers or for firms without an exchange member on the floor.
Infant Industry Clause	Clause used to justify import tariff protection, especially in developing countries, where an industry in the early stages of development could collapse if faced with direct competition from imports.
Insider Trading	Unlawful exploitation of inside or privileged information for profit in market transactions. More precisely in the USA, trading on the basis of material non-public information gained through an insider or privileged position.
Insolvent	Being unable to pay debts as they become due; not strictly the same as **Bankruptcy**.
Institutional Investors	Refers to institutions such as pension funds, investment trusts and insurance companies.
Institutional Pot	In the USA the share of a security offering specifically put aside for large institutional orders.
Intangible Assets	Items such as the cost of patents and trade marks, the legal costs of purchasing or starting a business and goodwill.
Interim Dividend	Distribution of profits made by a company in a trading period, usually part-yearly, e.g. quarterly, half-yearly. Authorised solely by a firm's directors. Seee **Final Dividend**.
Intermediate Goods	Goods used to produce other goods instead of being consumed themselves.
Internal Financing	Funds produced by a company's own operations and not derived from borrowing and new equity.
Internal Reserves	In the Japanese context, reserves after dividend payments and including contingency funds such as those for planned research and development spending in the coming year (these are sometimes included in capital spending). If funds

are insufficient to pay a dividend, these are put into internal reserves. See **Reserves**.

International Banking Facilities (IBF)

A means by which US banks may use their domestic offices to offer foreign customers deposit and loan facilities free of Federal Reserve Board reserve requirements and interest rate regulations. See **Offshore Banking Unit (OBU)**.

Investment Bank

US bank acting as an underwriter for new issues of stocks or bonds which as part of a syndicate redistributes the issue to investors. Also carries out other functions similar to a British merchant bank, such as advising clients.

Investment Management Regulatory Organisation (IMRO)

UK body that regulates fund management firms offering discretionary management services.

Investment Trust

Company engaged in buying securities of various kinds with a view to distributing the income to its shareholders.

Issued Capital

Authorised capital actually issued in the form of common, ordinary or preferred stock, based on the nominal value. See **Market Capitalisation**.

Jobber

See **Market Maker** and **Big Bang**.

Joint Stock Company

See **Public Limited Company (Plc)**.

Joint Venture

Cooperation between two or more companies or countries to produce mutually agreeable results from a particular project.

Legal List

List of investments in the USA selected by various states in which certain institutions, banks and insurance companies are allowed to invest.

Leverage

(a) Effect of the use of senior capital (bonds and preferred stock) over junior capital (common/ordinary stock) in capitalisations. High leverage can enable common/ordinary stockholders to benefit from an above-average level of profitability from employed loan stock, but it works to the company's detriment in a downturn since fixed charges must be met. See **Gearing**. (b) In commodities, it indicates the margin/capital ratio.

Leveraged Buyout (LBO)

When funds are raised to take over a company and that company's assets are used as collateral for the borrowing. The purchaser then repays the loans out of the acquired company's cash flow, or by selling its assets.

Leveraged Lease Provision by lender of only a small share of the cost of equipment being leased, the rest being provided by another lender.

Liabilities A company's debts and dividends to shareholders. Opposite of **Assets**.

LIFO Last in, first out. See **FIFO**.

Limited Liability Restriction of an owner's loss in a business to the amount of capital he has put into it.

Liquid Assets Also quick assets. Cash and readily disposable current assets.

Liquidation (a) Dissolution or winding up of a company, either voluntary or compulsory. (b) Disposal of assets for cash.

Liquidity Ratios Ratios which indicate a borrower's ability to meet short term obligations incurred. The ratio of liquid assets to current liabilities is described as the quick or acid test ratio on a company's balance sheet. See **Acid Test Ratio**.

Listing When a securities issue is listed on a stock exchange, it is approved for trading.

Lists Closed A list of applications to subscribe to an issue of securities is closed on a set date by those making the issue.

Lloyd's The Corporation of Lloyd's in London and the associated insurance market, where virtually any insurance proposal may be accepted for underwriting.

Loan Capital Part of a company's capital represented by loans from outside the company. Loan stock is long-term interest bearing stock issued by a firm, often as a debenture.

Loss Leader Goods sold by a trader at less than their cost in the hope of attracting enough profitable business to other products as compensation.

Margin In stock markets shares may be bought "on margin", the buyer having to pay only part of the purchase price in cash immediately, i.e. the customer uses his broker's credit. See **Stock Margin Trading** and entry under GENERAL MARKET TERMS.

Market Capitalisation (a) Total value of a company's securities at current prices—the total number of shares in issue multiplied by the market price. See **Issued Capital**. (b) The total valuation of all securities listed on a stock exchange or the total value of particular types of securities.

Market Maker	In Britain, for example, this is a Stock Exchange member firm which is prepared to buy or sell shares at all times, thus "making a market" in them and profiting from the spread. Before Big Bang, this role was filled by jobbers, who were not allowed to deal with the public. Post Big Bang, all members are broker/dealers, some of whom will specialise as market makers. See **Big Bang** and entry under GENERAL MARKET TERMS.

May Day	In the USA fixed minimum brokerage commissions ended on May 1, 1975. This led to diversification by the brokerage industry into a wide range of financial services using the latest in computers and communications systems.

Merchant Bank	Originally a bank which specialised in financing international trade and as such developed specialist knowledge of the countries with which it dealt. Now plays a much broader role by acting as an issuing house for stocks, bonds, by raising loans, equity capital, dealing in bills and foreign exchange. Merchant banks also act for and advise companies e.g. in merger situations, and some deal in bullion.

Merger	Fusion of two companies, or sometimes an acquisition or takeover of one company by another.

Minority Interest	Equity interest in a subsidiary company which is held outside the controlling parent company.

Minority Shareholders	Holders of the minority interest in a company.

Money Center Bank	Used in the USA to distinguish from regional banks. Refers to national banks in major world financial centres such as New York, London and Tokyo. They are large lenders to international governments and corporations as well as active buyers of money market instruments and securities.

Multinational	Company that has manufacturing bases or other forms of direct investment in several countries.

Multiples	Analytical equity ratios such as price/earnings ratio; a corporation stock price expressed as a multiple of reported earnings per share.

Mutual Fund	Open-end investment company i.e. one which continuously sells and redeems its shares. These shares are not traded on any exchange. See **Unit Trust**.

NASDAQ System	The National Association of Securities Dealers Automated Quotations system, owned and operated by the self-regulatory National Association of Securities Dealers (NASD). This computerised system provides price quotes for securities traded on the US Over the Counter (OTC) market as well as for many NYSE-listed securities.

Negotiable Order of Withdrawal (NOW Account)

Interest earning account in the USA on which technically only bank drafts may be drawn. In practice virtually a cheque account. May be owned only by individuals and certain non-profit organisations.

Net

Any figure from which some liability, such as tax, has been deducted. Thus a net dividend is one from which standard rate income tax has been deducted; net current assets are current assets minus current liabilities.

Net Asset Value

See **Book Value**.

Net Asset Worth

Measurement of value applied to ordinary shares and calculated by dividing the net equity assets by the number of ordinary shares.

Net Cash Flow

Retained earnings plus depreciation.

Net Equity Assets

Net assets less the repayment value of the preference capital including any arrears on interest.

Net Price Trading

If dealing with a UK market maker in the post-Big Bang era, this means that the deal is done at the selling (bid) price or the buying (offer) price, with no commission payable.

Net Profit

Trading profits after deducting the charges detailed in the profit and loss account. These include debits such as taxation, depreciation, auditors' and directors' fees. In Japan, net profit is net of tax and other items including extraordinaries and before deductions for certain special reserves, dividend payments and internal reserves.

Net Sales

Gross sales less allowances, discounts etc.

Net Working Capital

Current assets net of current liabilities.

Net Worth

Total assets net of total liabilities. Equivalent to capital.

New Time Dealing

Dealing for "new time" on the London Stock Exchange during the two days preceding the next accounting period. This enables payment for the deal to be deferred until the settlement days of the following account.

Nil Paid

A new issue of shares, usually as the result of a rights issue, on which no payment to the company has yet been made.

No Par Value

Stocks without face, or nominal, value.

Nominal Capital	See **Authorised Capital/Stock**.
Non-Performance Loan	Loans where the borrower has failed to pay on time or in the full amount.
Non-Resident Account	Account owned by a person who is not a resident of the country where the account is held.
Non-Voting Stock	Securities that do not allow the holder to vote on company resolutions or elect directors.
Nostro Account	Bank's account with a foreign bank, e.g. a US bank's account in Germany with a German Bank. See **Vostro Account**.
NSCC	See entry under ECONOMY, CURRENCY.
NYSE Common Stock Index	Composite index covering all stocks listed on the New York Stock Exchange, based on the market close at end of December 1965 as 50.00 and weighted according to the number of shares listed for each issue. There are four supplementary indices for industrials, transportation, utilities and finance.
Off Balance Sheet Activities	Banks' business, often fee-based, that does not generally involve booking assets and taking deposits. Examples are trading of swaps, options and letters of credit.
Offer Document	Official document from the bidder in a takeover battle sent to shareholders in the target company.
Offshore Banking Unit (OBU)	A foreign bank usually handling foreign exchange, Eurocurrency and domestic money market transactions in a centre where the capital market is free and enjoys advantages in terms of tax and/or reserve requirements. See **International Banking Facilities (IBF)**.
Offshore Centre	Conglomeration of OBUs drawn together by the tax advantages of operating in that centre e.g. Bahrain, Cayman Islands.
Offshore Funds	Funds based outside the tax system of the country in which intended investors reside.
Operating Profit (Loss)	The after tax earnings from a company's ordinary revenue-producing activities. Precise definitions vary. In West Germany the "Betriebsergebnis" of commercial banks covers profit before tax, writedowns and risk provisions. In Japan, operating profit is before tax and after the costs of production, administration and sales.
Optional Dividend	Payment, which the shareholder can choose to receive in either cash or stock form.

Ordinary Capital Capital in a company which is entitled to the residue (or equity) of profits and assets after senior capital issues, such as preference or preferred ordinary shares, as well as creditors and others outside the business have received their due.

Ordinary Dividend Part of the profit accruing to the ordinary capital which is distributed to its holders. In the USA also called common dividend.

Ordinary Shares Fully-paid shares ranking after debentures and preference shares for dividend payments. Ordinary shareholders usually have voting rights.

Over The Counter (OTC) (a) Method of trading shares which for one reason or another do not meet the requirements of trading on a main stock exchange but are bought and sold in a secondary market, i.e. over the counter. (b) Market conducted directly between dealers and principals via a telephone and computer network, rather than via a highly-regulated exchange trading floor.

Paid Up Capital Shares for which the company has received the full nominal value in payment. No further liabilities attach to the shareholders. See **Partly Paid, Nil Paid**.

Paper Profit Apparent profit arising out of an unrealised increase in the value of an asset.

Par See entry under LENDING.

Participating Preference Capital Capital whose holders are entitled not only to the receipts of a fixed interest payment out of profits but also, in certain defined circumstances, to a share in the balance of the profits.

Participation Certificates (a) In Switzerland, a non-voting form of equity issued by Swiss companies. (b) In USA, an interest in a pool of funds.

Pari Passu Latin for "with equal progress". When a new issue of shares is made, they rank "pari passu" or equally with existing shares for dividend payments.

Partly Paid Shares for which the full nominal value has not been paid and on which a liability to pay the balance exists. Often used in connection with new issues when the terms of the issue require only part of the issue price to be paid on application. See **Paid Up Capital**.

Passing Dividend No dividend payments authorised by the company due to a lack of, or insufficient, profits.

P/E Ratio Price/earnings ratio. The current market price of a company's stock expressed as a multiple of its total per share earnings for the previous 12 months.

Pension Funds Funds invested by the state, trade union or corporate sector for their members' pensions. An important source of finance for the capital market and investment. Pension funds can have a considerable impact on the stock markets, as well as on economic activity.

Percentage Earnings Profit expressed as a percentage of the nominal capital employed.

Ploughed Back Earnings Profit which is not distributed but reinvested in the company.

Poison Pill When a company is in danger of being taken over against its wishes, it may plot moves to make its stock less attractive. One such move would be to issue new preferred stock giving shareholders the right of redemption at a premium after any takeover. Since this strategy in effect raises the cost of an acquisition, the potential predator may be deterred from going ahead. See **Shark Repellant**.

Portfolio Through holding a "portfolio", an investor aims to reduce risk by diversifying into a number of shares in differing companies and/or combining shareholdings with other assets such as bonds or money market instruments.

Pre-emptive Right Right of shareholders and others to maintain their proportional control of, and equity in a corporation when additional shares are issued.

Preferential Form The London Stock Exchange allows companies offering shares to the public to set aside up to 10 per cent of the issue for applications from employees, or, when a parent company is floating off a subsidiary, shareholders of the parent company.

Preferential Debts See entry under LENDING.

Preferred Stock/ Shares Fixed dividend shares which have a prior asset claim over common stock shares. Ordinary or common shareholders cannot receive full dividends until preferred dividends have been paid in full. Similarly, they rank behind preference shareholders for claims on any assets of a company when it is wound up.

Price/Earnings Ratio See **P/E Ratio**.

Primary Earnings Per Share

US net income divided by the number of outstanding common shares plus common stock equivalents.

Prior Charges

Charges on debentures, loan stock, notes etc. which rank ahead of share capital. The service of interest on such charges is a cost of running the company which must be met before any dividend is paid, and in the event of default on the conditions of the issue the repayment of such indebtedness is a charge ranking before share capital.

Priority Percentage

Apportionment of profit earned in any year which is required to service the different classes of capital expressed, in order of priority, as a percentage of the amount available.

Privatisation

A word popularised after the 1979 election of British Prime Minister Margaret Thatcher to illustrate her Conservative Party's intention of putting efficient government-owned services into private hands.

Profit And Loss Account

An account showing a company's earnings and expenses over a period, what it has done with its profits, how much is being paid out in dividends and how much is retained for the company.

Profit Margin

Net profit as a percentage of sales or capital.

Profit Participation Certificates

West German non-voting certificates (Genussscheine) offering an annual payment based on profits. They can be of unlimited duration or, like a bond, have a fixed life.

Program Trading

Computer-based trading techniques relying e.g. in the stock market on factors such as the flow of trading, current prices and movements in futures and options rather than on responses to corporate earnings or economic indicators. Program trading also aims to exploit arbitrage possibilities between US stock index futures/options and underlying equities.

Prospectus

Document offering and giving details of a new issue of stock or debt.

Proxy

Person or legal entity authorised to represent, and if necessary act and vote on behalf of another.

Pty Ltd

Australian term. A Proprietary Limited (Pty Ltd) company is a private company (or a subsidiary of a publicly-listed one) which can neither invite the public to subscribe for its shares nor take deposits from the public. However, firms designated as Pty Co Ltd are listed.

Public Limited Company (Plc) UK term denoting a publicly held rather than a privately owned limited company. Formerly known as Joint Stock Company.

Public Utilities State or private sector enterprises providing services of public interest, e.g. gas, electricity, water, telecommunications.

Quoted Company One listed on an official stock exchange; its shares are "quoted" and available for trading to the general public.

Raider Investor, generally hostile, aiming to buy a controlling interest in a company's stock and install new management. In the USA raiders acquiring at least five per cent of the targeted corporation shares must report their purchases to the Securities and Exchange Commission, the exchange where the stock is listed, and to the company itself. Sometimes the raider simply aims to buy part of the target company's stock and then sell it for a quick profit.

Real Estate Investment Trust (REIT) US property development and investment company.

Receivables Outstanding debts due to a corporation.

Receiver In a form of bankruptcy, the receiver generally manages—at a court's behest—the affairs of a troubled business for the benefit of its owners and creditors, until debts are paid or a court settlement is reached. See **Bankruptcy** and **Liquidation**.

Registered Security Security registered on the books of the issuing company in the name of the owner. Such ownership can only be transferred when endorsed by the owner.

Registration Requirement for a corporation to be listed in the USA under the 1934 Securities Exchange Act before it can be admitted for dealings on a national security exchange. Public offerings of new securities by a corporation or outstanding securities by controlling shareholders must also be registered under the 1933 Securities Act. Similar rules with basically the same objectives exist in countries where there are exchanges and securities markets. However, the exact amount of information which must be disclosed and the different legal requirements can vary considerably between countries.

Regular Way Delivery System in the US stock and bond markets whereby securities sold must be delivered by the selling broker to the purchasing broker and payment made by the fifth business day after the sale. Government bonds must be delivered the next business day after the transaction.

Regulated Market A new tier of West German stock exchange trading (der geregelte Markt), similar to London's Unlisted Securities Market (USM). See **Unlisted Securities Market (USM)**.

Reinsurer Insurance concern operating in the reinsurance market whereby the initial insurer reinsures or shares part of the original risk.

Reserves Shareholder's funds, held as cash or in highly liquid assets, which consist primarily of profits retained in the business and accumulated over the years rather than paid out by way of dividends to shareholders. This segregation of retained earnings can be used to provide for later payouts of dividends, or for other contingencies, improvements or retirement of preferred stock.

Restricted Transferability Swiss company statutes provide for restricted transferability (in German, Vinkulierung) of registered shares, giving management the right to refuse voting rights to unwanted shareholders.

Repatriation Restoration of financial assets from abroad to the home nation.

Restructuring Change in a company's asset and cost structure. Sometimes used by companies applying to a court to come out of bankruptcy, sometimes used by firms attempting to raise the price of their shares and thus escape being taken over.

Retail Banking Provision of banking services to individuals and small businesses; includes deposit facilities, lending and fund transferrals. Compares with **Wholesale Banking**.

Retained Profits Profits earned for the equity holders in a company which are not distributed as a dividend to shareholders. Accumulated retained profits are reserves on the balance sheet. See **Reserves**.

Rights Privileged stock or bond offering below market prices usually offered to existing shareholders or loan subscribers. A new offering on this basis is known as a rights issue.

Risk Arbitrageurs Traders attempting to profit from an expected rise in the price of a takeover target's shares and a drop in the price of the bidder's shares. Such traders simultaneously buy stock in the former and sell shares in the latter. They also invest in a takeover target, if they think the bidder will be forced to raise his price.

Risk Capital Money invested in a business or project which offers a lower than usual likelihood of profit, but if successful a big return.

Royalty	Payment by a person or company to the owner of property or creator of original work for the privilege of using it commercially. See entry under ENERGY.
Run	Process of widening, cumulative demands on a bank or other financial institution, seeking the return of funds or money deposited with it.
Run-Up	US term for a quick rise in a security's price.
Scrip	Subscription certificate. Used for a provisional document given to a person allotted shares. Also, more widely, any form of security.
Scrip Issue	See **Capitalisation Issue**.
SEAQ	Britain's Stock Exchange Automated Quotation service, operative in the post-Big Bang era. It is a screen-based dealing system, on which the competing market makers in any particular security display their buying and selling prices simultaneously to all users of the system.
Secondary Offering	Also known as a secondary distribution. The redistribution in the USA of a block of stock, normally of an established corporation, some time after it has been brought to market by a firm or group of securities firms. Normally a block too large to be absorbed by the market in the regular course of trading.
Securities	General name for stocks and shares of all types. In common usage stocks are fixed interest securities, while shares are the rest.
Securities And Exchange Commission (SEC)	Official US body established by the Securities Exchange Act of 1934. Charged with regulatory oversight and administering rules associated with all parts of the securities industry.
Securities And Investments Board (SIB)	The top UK regulatory body established under the 1986 Financial Services Act to oversee the investment business, mainly through five satellite self-regulatory organisations (SROs). See **Self-Regulatory Organisation (SRO)**.
Self-Regulatory Organisation (SRO)	Private organisation set up by a market itself to watch over trading activities.
Settlement Day	See **Account Day**.
Share	A security which represents a portion of the owner's capital in a business. A person who buys a portion of a company's

capital becomes a shareholder in that company's assets and receives a share of any company profit in dividend form.

Share Capital Total of shares authorised to be issued, or actually issued by a company. See **Paid Up Capital**.

Share Premium Premium charged on the issue of shares in excess of their nominal value.

Share Register Register kept by a limited company giving details of shareholders, including addresses of shareholders.

Shark Repellent A company move to discourage an unwanted takeover. See **Poison Pill**.

Shelf Registration Occurs when companies register securities they intend to issue in the future when market conditions are deemed to be favourable.

Shell Company Small company with a stockmarket quote but few other assets.

SIAC Securities Industry Automation Corporation. An independent organisation established by the New York and American Stock Exchanges as a jointly-owned subsidiary to provide automated data processing, clearing and communications services.

SIPC Securities Investor Protection Corporation. Established in the USA in 1970 to protect securities firms' customers from losses resulting from securities firms' financial failure. All US broker dealers are requested to be members.

Smokestack Industries Heavy industries such as steel and car production.

Soft Goods Non-durables such as consumer or producer goods with a limited life.

Special Bid Method of filing an order to buy a large block of stock on the floor of the New York Stock Exchange. The bidder pays a special commission to the broker representing him but the seller does not pay a commission. The special bid is made on the floor of the exchange at a fixed price which may not be below the last sale of the security or the current regular market, whichever is the higher.

Spin Off Method used by a company to split its operations and assets by proportionately distributing to its own shareholders shares which it owns in another company. Sometimes called hive off.

Split/Stock Split	Division of the outstanding shares of a corporation into a larger number of shares, although the proportional ownership of the shares is maintained.
Stag	Operator who applies for a new security on the chance of selling it on allotment at a premium over the issue price.
Stock Dividend	Authorised but unissued shares paid to shareholders as a dividend.
Stock Exchange	Organised trading floor for stock and share transactions.
Stock Margin Trading	In Japan, for example, there is a six-month lag between buying a share "on margin" and the compulsory settlement (selling) of that share. Since such trading is speculative and volatile, regular reports on it serve to alert investors to what may happen in six months time. See **Margin**.
Stock Option	Contract conferring the right to all or certain employees to buy or sell a specified number of shares at a certain price in a stipulated period.
Stock-Sales Ratio	Ratio of inventory stocks to turnover, measuring buoyancy in the business economy.
Striking Price	Price at which shares are allotted in a UK tender offer for sale. Everyone tendering at or above the striking price gets some shares at that price. Those tendering below, don't.
Subsidiary	A company under the control of another company which owns all or most of it.
Sunrise Industries	High-technology manufacturing industries which are heavily automated and regarded by many as the mainstays of the future economy.
Subscription	Purchase of newly-issued securities.
Synergy	Occurs in the merger of two companies, if the performance of the combined enterprise is greater than that of the previously separate parts.
Take Down	To receive and accept an allotment of shares or bonds in the primary market.
Takeover	Acquisition of a controlling interest in one company by another through the purchase of its shares.
Takeover Panel	A self-regulatory UK body which sets and polices the rules for takeovers. Known officially as the Panel on Takeovers and Mergers.

TALISMAN Transfer Accounting, Lodging for Investors and Stock Management for Jobbers. This is the London Stock Exchange's computerised settlement system.

Ten (10) K Detailed corporate annual reporting form required by the US Securities and Exchange Commission. Basically similar but supplementary to the annual report.

Tender Offer In the USA a public offer to buy shares for cash or other securities from existing shareholders of one corporation by another company or organisation under specified terms in force for a limited period. In the UK the offer for sale, in which investors are asked to bid for stock in order to determine the striking price at which the shares will be actually sold.

The Securities Association (TSA) Regulates the London Stock Exchange and the international bond dealing community.

Throughput See entry under ENERGY.

Times Covered Number of times the amount available for distribution, i.e. company earnings, can be divided by the amount of the distribution, i.e. dividend.

Trading Post A structure on the floor of the New York Stock Exchange at which stocks or options are bought and sold.

Treasury Stock In the USA stock issued by a company but later reacquired. It can be held, retired or reissued. While held by the company, it does not receive a dividend and cannot be used for voting purposes.

Turnkey Order Order for an industrial plant which is completely operational when it is handed over to the buyer.

Undercapitalisation When a business has not been supplied with enough funds by its owners to support its activities and herald expansion.

Unit Trust British equivalent of a mutual fund. It invests the combined contributions from many people in various securities and pays them dividends in proportion to their holdings. See **Mutual Fund**.

Unitary Wage Rate Average hourly wage rate paid to a blue-collar worker in the US manufacturing industry.

Universal Bank Large banks in West Germany and Switzerland which have traditionally conducted both commercial and investment banking. They also often own large stakes in industrial companies.

Unlisted Security

Security that is not listed or traded on the stock exchange floor.

Unlisted Securities Market (USM)

In London the Stock Exchange admits newer and smaller companies to its USM. Although not given the status of a "listed company", they sign a general undertaking which binds them to very similar standards of disclosure (of information to investors).

Venture Capital

Also called **Risk Capital**. Funds used for investment in companies where there is a degree of financial risk in the initial stages, e.g. companies exploiting new technical processes.

Venture Capital Holding Companies

German firms (Unternehmungsbeteiligungsgesellschaften UBGG) taking stakes in small unlisted companies to provide them with external capital.

Voluntary Liquidation

See **Bankruptcy**.

Vostra Account

Account maintained abroad by a bank in the currency of the country in which the account is held. The bank holding the account would refer to it as a vostro account while the bank depositing it would refer to it as a **Nostra Account**.

Voting Rights

Most ordinary shares/common stock have equal rights to vote on matters affecting a company.

Warrant

See entry under LENDING.

White Knight

Rescues the target of an unfriendly takeover bid from the unwanted bidder. A white squire acts much the same, except that he only takes a large stake in the target rather than seeks control of it.

Wholesale Banking

Borrowing and lending activities among major corporations, banks, merchant banks and money market operators. See **Retail Banking**.

Windfall Profit

Unexpected profit.

Window Dressing

Steps by banks and companies to present their accounts in a favourable light, often by raising additional short term funds.

Withholding Tax

Tax on interest or dividend payments remitted to persons residing outside the country levying the tax; also tax deducted at source.

Working Capital   Surplus of current assets over current liabilities, which provides the net resources with which a company can finance day-to-day operations.

Working Control   Number of shares needed to control the activities of a corporation. In theory this is 51 per cent of all voting shares. In practice it can be less, sometimes considerably less, due to the distribution of stock ownership.

Write Down   To reduce the value of an asset by taking account of depreciation, or some other significant erosion of the asset's value.

Write Off   Book-keeping action which, at one stroke, depreciates an asset out of the balance sheet of a corporation or bank.

Commodities

ABRASSUCOS
Associação Brasileira das Indústrias de Sucos Cítricos.
Brazilian Association of Citrus Juice Industries.

ACP States
A group of 66 African, Caribbean and Pacific states associated with the European Community through the Lomé convention—a trade and aid agreement first signed in 1975 and renewable every five years.

Acreage Allotment
US government limitation on the planted acreage of some crops.

Acreage Reduction Program (ARP)
US government programme under which farmers are required to reduce planted acreage by a fixed percentage set by the Agriculture Secretary in order to be eligible for government crop support schemes such as the loan programme. See **Loan Rate, Marketing Loan** and **Set-Aside**.

ACSA
American Cotton Shippers Association.

Actuals
Also called **Physicals**. Refers to the physical commodities available for shipment, storage, manufacture. Physicals which are available for delivery are traded for cash on a spot or forward basis as opposed to futures contracts, which are traded on **Margin**.

Aflatoxin
Carcinogen produced e.g. by mould on stored maize.

Afloats
Commodities on board, underway, ready to sail.

Against Actuals
See **Exchange For Physical (EFP)**.

Agricultural Stabilization And Conservation Service (ASCS)
The US Department of Agriculture's main administrative arm with offices in every agricultural producing county. It is responsible for signing up producers for agriculture programmes and keeping track of participation. The ASCS also monitors US-owned farm stocks and sets prices for payment in kind redemption rates. See **Payment In Kind**.

Allowances
Discounts or premiums to par allowed for commodity grades or delivery locations which differ from the basis grade or location specified in a futures contract. See **Differentials**.

Aluminium
The most widely used metal after iron (including steel), it is a light base metal commonly employed in the construction industry. It is resistant to corrosion, a good conductor and easily workable. Major producers include the USA, Canada and the Soviet Union.

Animal Feed Ingredients	These include: (a) Manioc (tapioca or cassava). A root crop with a high energy value. (b) Maize gluten or corn gluten. A by-product from maize starch extraction, with high protein content. (c) Molasses. Mainly a binding agent for dry feedstuffs, also improves palatability. It is produced when making sugar from cane and sorghum. (d) Brans and sharps. Residues derived from milling cereals and having a similar nutritive composition to wheat and barley grains. (e) Fruitwaste, especially citrus. A dry concentrate made from the peel, pith and seed of fresh fruits. Its large amount of nitrogen-free extract makes it an attractive energy source.
Approved Delivery Facility	Any bank, stockyard, mill, store, warehouse, plant, elevator or other depositary recognised by an exchange as approved for the delivery of commodities tendered against a future contract.
Arabica/Robusta	Types of coffee bean with different tastes or "cupping quality". Broadly speaking, Arabica has a milder flavour and is regarded as being of better quality; it is grown predominantly in Central and South America but also in East Africa and India. Robusta is cultivated in French-speaking West African countries, Uganda, Zaïre and Indonesia. Instant coffee manufacturers use a blend of Arabica and Robusta coffees to achieve the required taste.
ASA	American Soybean Association.
ASPA	American Soybean Processors Association.
Aspartame	A non-caloric artificial sweetener.
Assay	To test qualitatively and quantitatively the purity of metals. The former is mainly used to assess the fineness of precious metals, and the latter by mining companies in assessing the potential of ore bodies.
Association Of Futures Brokers And Dealers (AFBD)	A self-regulatory organisation (SRO) with the specific responsibility for regulating the futures and options industry in the UK under the Financial Services Act.
Association Of Tin Producing Countries (ATPC)	Group comprising Malaysia, Thailand, Indonesia, Australia, Bolivia, Nigeria and Zaïre—with Brazil and China attending meetings as observers. It has operated supply controls to support tin prices and reduce stocks.
Authenticity	In the gold markets, the actual gold content of any lot in hand and authenticated by a reliable seller.
Backpricing	Price-fixing device in the metal market whereby a consumer with a long-term contract has the option of fixing the price

121

for a proportion of his contract on the valid London Metal Exchange settlement price. The LME settlement price is established at the close of the second morning ring and is accepted as the cash market price for the next 24 hours.

Backwardation A situation where the commodity's cash or near delivery price is at a premium to the price for forward delivery, i.e. opposite to contango. (It is used in the same way on foreign exchange markets). backwardation is often caused by delays in shipment, thus creating shortages in available supplies. See **Inverted Market**.

Bagasse The residue from crushing sugar cane.

Baltic Futures Exchange (BFE) Formed by bringing together all London futures markets which are physically situated on the Baltic Exchange, the traditional centre for dry cargo shipping. It includes the Baltic International Freight Futures Exchange (BIFFEX), the Soy Bean Meal Futures Association (SOMFA), the London Meat Futures Exchange (LMFE), the London Potato Futures Association (LPFA) and the London Grain Futures Market (LGFM). See entry **Baltic Exchange** under SHIPPING.

Barley Second to corn (maize) as major world feedgrain. It is also used in the brewing process for alcoholic drinks, and as a food grain.

Basis Difference between the cash price of a commodity at a specific location and the price of a particular futures contract—term used widely in the USA.

Basis Grade Grade of a commodity used as the standard of the contract.

Borrowing Used mainly in the London Metal Exchange to refer to the purchase of a nearby delivery date and simultaneous sale of a forward date. See **Lending**.

Bourse De Commerce Familiar term for the Paris commodity exchange.

Bourse De Commerce Européenne European Commodities Exchanges Association.

Bran The outer covering of a kernel of grain, also called the hull, which is mostly fibrous material.

Buffer Stock Stock of commodities held by an international organisation to stabilise prices and supplies by buying and selling, using the stockpile's resources.

Buffer Stock Financing Facility (BSFF) — Facility which can be used by IMF member countries in balance of payments difficulties to draw up to 50 per cent of their IMF quota to finance contributions to international buffer stock arrangements.

Bullion — Precious metal in non-coined form, i.e. ingots, bars or wafers.

Bushel — Measure of capacity. In the UK it equals eight Imperial gallons or 36.4 litres for corn, fruit, liquids etc. In the USA it equals 35.3 litres. The weight of a bushel varies according to the commodity involved.

Cairns Group — Group of 13 agricultural free trading nations, including Argentina, Australia, Brazil, Canada and New Zealand. it has proposed separate plans for reforming world agriculture to those put forward by the USA and the European Community.

Car Or Carload — Term used in US commodity trading for a load of railway freight car.

Carat — Measure of the fineness of gold. Pure gold is 24 carats, i.e. there is no alloy. Thus 19 carat gold represents 19 parts gold and five parts alloy. It is also used as a measure of weight for precious stones, when it equals 200 milligrams.

Carries — A London Metal Exchange term for simultaneous matching purchase of one delivery with the sale of another. In other markets called straddles or switches. See **Spread**.

Carrying Charge — (a) Cost of storing a physical commodity including insurance, storage and interest charges. (b) Full carrying charge market. A situation in the futures market when price differentials between delivery months fully reflect insurance, storage and interest costs.

Carryover — Part of current crop production carried over into the next crop year, or that part of current supplies of a commodity comprising stocks from the previous year's production. See entry under EQUITIES.

Carteira Do Comércio Exterior Do Banco Do Brasil S.A. (CACEX) — Export trade department of the commercial Banco do Brasil. Registers exports of several Brazilian commodities such as soy and orange juice.

Cash And Carry — Simultaneous purchase of a commodity for cash delivery and sale of the same commodity for delivery at a later date.

Cash Commodity — Physical commodity as distinct from a futures contract.

Cash Crop   A crop grown for sale rather than for food.

Cash Market   The trading of physical commodities as opposed to contracts on a futures exchange. Also sometimes referred to as the spot market, which for some commodities means trading for nearby delivery, while in others spot market encompasses nearby as well as forward physical deals. See **Spot** under GENERAL MARKET TERMS and **Spot Market** under ENERGY.

Cash Settlement   Settlement of maturing futures market contracts in cash rather than by delivery of the physical commodity.

CBOE   Chicago Board Options Exchange, an affiliate of the Chicago Board of Trade. It proclaims itself the world's first and largest securities options exchange.

CBOT/CBT   See **Chicago Board Of Trade**.

Cereals   Edible grains. These are wheat, oats, barley, rye, rice, maize (corn), millet and sorghum.

Certificated (Or Certified) Stock   Stocks which have been inspected and approved as deliverable quality against futures contracts. In grains, stocks in a deliverable position.

CFTC   Commodity Futures Trading Commission. Established by the US Congress to administer the 1974 Commodity Futures Trading Act. It has jurisdiction over all commodities contract markets in the USA. It comrpises five commissioners, one of whom is designated chairman. All are appointed by the President. They are subject to Senate confirmation and independent of all government departments.

Chicago Board Of Trade (CBOT)   A major exchange for financial futures and options, metal futures and options, agricultural futures and options, and equity index futures.

Chicago Mercantile Exchange (CME)   A major commodities futures exchange for livestock and financial instruments. Also known as the "Merc". (In energy markets "Merc" refers to the New York Mercantile Exchange or Nymex which trades heating oil and gasoline futures). See **NYMEX** under ENERGY.

CICILS   Confédération Internationale du Commerce et des Industries des Légumes Secs (the International Confederation of Pulse Trade and Industry) based in Paris.

Class, Wheat   There are five official basic classes of US wheat: Hard Red Spring, Hard Red Winter, Durum, Soft Red Winter and White.

Coarse Grains   E.g. maize, barley, sorghum, oats, rye and millet. See **Fine Grains**.

COCERAL	Comité du Commerce des Céréales et des Aliments du Bétail de la CEE (Committee for Trade in Cereals and Animal Feed in the EC), the community's main cereal lobby.
Cocoa	Crop producing beans which contain 50–57 per cent fat called cocoa butter. In the manufacture of powder for drinking, the fat is largely removed, but in making chocolate, extra cocoa butter is added. Cocoa butter is also used in some cosmetics.
Cocoa Shipment Declaration	Confirms to the buyer in an official document that his contracted purchase is being shipped, giving bill of lading details and the number of bags he is to receive. See **Bill Of Lading** under SHIPPING.
Coconut Oil	Lauric vegetable oil extracted from Copra.
Coffee	Major importers are industrialised countries such as the United States and the European Community, although Brazil, the largest producer, is also one of the main consumers. The International Coffee Organization divides world exports into the following categories: Colombian Milds—mostly Colombian coffee but also Kenyan and Tanzanian; Other Milds—Central America, Ecuador, Peru, Papua New Guinea and some Indian output; Arabica and Robusta. See **Arabica/Robusta** and **International Coffee Organization**.
Coffee Rust	Serious fungus disease attacking coffee plants resulting in them losing leaves, thus reducing the coffee yield. After a number of years, the affected plants die.
Coffee, Sugar And Cocoa Exchange (CSCE)	New York futures market trading coffee, sugar and cocoa contracts.
COGECA	Comité Générale de la Coopération Agricole des Pays de la Communauté (General Committee for Agricultural Cooperation in the EC).
Colza	See **Rapeseed**.
Comex	Commodity Exchange Inc. A New York commodity futures market trading principally in gold, silver and copper.
Commission House	Concern that buys and sells actual commodities or futures contracts for the accounts of customers, i.e. its income is generated by the commission charged for its service.
Commodity Credit Corporation (CCC)	US government agency, set up in 1933, responsible for directing and financing major US Department of Agriculture action programmes including price support and production adjustment. It also directs and finances agricultural export

activities, including credit sales, barter deals, export payments and foreign food aid.

Commodity Exchange

Market in which commodity futures are bought and sold. Major exchanges include those in London, Chicago, New York, Paris, Sydney, Hong Kong, Kuala Lumpur, Tokyo and Singapore. Delivery of the underlying commodity may also take place.

Commodity Stabilisation Agreements

International agreements involving producers, and in some cases consumers, in efforts to stabilise production and/or prices of commodities.

Common Agricultural Policy (CAP)

The EC system aimed at guaranteeing farmers' incomes by bridging the gap between world market prices for major commodities and the normally higher prices set by the EC, through a complex of price support mechanisms, export restitutions, social and other measures.

Common Fund

UN Conference on Trade and Development (UNCTAD) Common Fund for Commodities. Negotiated in 1980, the fund was originally conceived as a central pool of finance that could be drawn on by international commodity agreements to help keep market prices stable through buffer stock operations. UNCTAD recently has put more emphasis on the fund's "second window" which provides finance for research, development, marketing and diversification. Only international bodies representing both consumers and producers are eligible for second window funds.

Companhia De Financiamento Da Produção (CFP)

Brazilian Production Financing Company. A Brazilian government agency which advises the government on minimum support prices and levels of financing for farmers of grains, oilseeds and various other crops. It also holds government stocks of these commodities and takes advantage of its network of offices throughout the Brazilian interior to assess progress and quantity of crops. It can also hold import and export tenders for some commodities.

Co-Responsibility Levy

European Community "tax" on farm producers to help pay for storing and disposing of surpluses.

Conillon

Brazilian variety of Robusta coffee—see **Arabica/Robusta**.

Consejo Inter-gubernamental De Paises Exportadores De Cobre (CIPEC)

Paris-based Intergovernmental Council of Copper Exporting Countries. Members are Australia, Chile, Indonesia, Papua New Guinea, Peru, Yugoslavia, Zaïre and Zambia.

Conservation Reserve Program (CRP)
Programme under which the US government pays farmers to keep cropland fallow or idle for 10 years.

Contango
A situation where prices are higher in the forward delivery months than in the nearby delivery month, i.e. opposite of backwardation. A contango normally occurs when supplies are adequate or in surplus. The higher prices reflect, either wholly or in part, the costs of holding and financing. See entry under EQUITIES.

Contract
On commodity markets the precise specifications, e.g. price, delivery point and delivery date laid down by a futures market to denote a standard trading unit.

Contract Grades (Units)
Standard set for each commodity which must be observed when commodities are delivered against futures contracts. Most contracts have a number of grades or qualities which result in a premium or discount when delivery actually takes place.

Contract Month
Month in which delivery is due under a futures contract, i.e. when the contract matures.

Contract Trading Volume
Total number of contracts traded in a commodity or a commodity delivery month during a specific period.

COPA
Comité des Organisations Professionelles Agricoles de la Communauté (the Committee for Professional Agricultural Organisations in the EC), i.e. federation of EC farm unions.

Copper
Base metal mined chiefly in Chile, Zambia, Zaïre, USA, Canada, USSR, Peru, Philippines and Australasia. It is used mostly in the electrical, engineering and building industries.

Copra
Dried kernels of coconut.

Corn (Or Maize)
Major world feed grain for animals. It is used to yield edible vegetable oil, alcohol, high fructose corn syrup (HFCS), corn gluten feed for animals and products for human consumption, such as corn meal and corn flour.

Corn Gluten Feed
Corn (maize) meal. A byproduct used in animal feed. See **Animal Feed Ingredients**.

Cotton Gin
Machinery separating the cottonseed and foreign materials from cotton fibres.

Cottonseed Oil, Meal
Oil is extracted from cottonseed chemically or by crushing. The residue becomes cottonseed meal and is used as animal feed.

Cover

On commodities markets the purchase/sale of futures to offset a previously established short/long position.

Crop Year

Time period from the start of one harvest to the next, varying according to the commodity and country, e.g. 1 June to 31 May for US wheat, 1 September to 31 August for US soybeans. The Bangladesh cotton crop year runs from sowing to harvest, i.e. July to February. See **New Crop** and **Old Crop**.

Crush Margin

The price difference between the value of oilseeds such as soybeans and the value of the end products, oil and meal.

Crush Spread

A futures deal where a trader buys soybeans and sells the same amount of meal and oil that the beans would produce. Reverse is known as a reverse crush.

Crushing Subsidy

In the European Community, oilseed producers' returns are maintained by a subsidy paid to crushers to bridge the gap between (normally) lower world prices and higher EC support prices.

Custom Smelter

A smelter which relies on concentrate purchased from independent mines instead of its own captive sources.

Dead Rent

In mining leases rent which is payable whether a mine is worked or not.

Decoupling

A concept which urges that payments to farmers be separated from direct effects on production and market prices. Under decoupling, payment would be made to farmers regardless of production, making farm subsidies more of a social programme than an economic one.

Default

(a) Failure of a party under a futures contract to fulfil the contract requirements or failure to make or take delivery of the physical commodity in the futures market. (b) Decision by a farmer, under the US farm loan programme, to surrender his crops rather than repay a government loan. See entry under LENDING.

Deferred Futures

Distant months of a futures contract. See **Nearbys**.

Deferred Pricing

Sales contract condition for cash grain, where agreement is made for price terms to be set at a future date.

Deficiency Payments

(a) System of supporting farm product prices used in the UK before it joined the EC. It involved payments to farmers of the difference between average free market prices for certain products and guaranteed prices (normally higher) fixed annually. (b) In the USA, deficiency payments are made by the government to farmers who participate in feedgrain, wheat, rice or cotton programmes. They are based on the difference between a target price and the domestic market price or loan rate, whichever is the less. See **Loan Rate**.

Deliverable Grades	See **Contract Grades**.
Delivery	Tender and receipt of the actual commodity or financial instrument or in settlement of a futures contract.
Delivery Month	Month in which a futures contract matures and becomes deliverable.
Delivery Notice	Written notice from a clearing house of seller's intention to deliver the actual commodity against his open short futures position. Also known in the USA as "issues and stops".
Delivery Points	Locations where stocks of commodities or financial instruments represented by futures contracts may be delivered in fulfilment of contract. The commodity exchanges designate the specific locations.
Delivery Price	Settlement price set by a clearing house for deliveries of commodities against futures contracts.
Denatured Wheat	Wheat treated under the EC Common Agricultural Policy to make it unfit for human consumption. The intention is to stop it qualifying for a bread wheat subsidy.
Dextrose	Sugar substitute obtained from corn starch.
Differentials	Discounts or premiums permitted when delivering a commodity of different standard or at different location from that specified in the futures contract. See **Allowances**.
Discount	(a) The difference between prices quoted for nearer position and those more distant. (b) The lowering of the price allowed for delivery of stocks of a commodity below contract grade against a futures contract.
Dockage	Waste and foreign material found in grains and oilseeds when grading takes place.
Double Option	Commodity term for the option to buy and sell.
Durum Wheat	Hard wheat used in making pasta.
Elevators	See **Public Elevators**.
Equity	In the US commodities markets, the remaining value of a futures trading account, if it is disposed of at current market prices. See entry under EQUITIES.

European Agricultural Guidance And Guarantee Fund (EAGGF)	Also known by its French abbreviation FEOGA. The trust fund is used to finance the EC's Common Agricultural Policy.
Even Lot	Commodity trading unit governed by official exchange price quotations.
Exchange For Physical (EFP)	Also called exchange for cash. A situation where the buyer of a cash commodity transfers to the seller an equivalent amount of long futures contracts, or receives from him a corresponding amount of short futures at an agreed price.
Execution By Outcry	Commodity exchange orders transacted by oral offer and acceptance in the trading ring or pit.
Ex Pit Transactions	Trades executed outside the exchange trading ring or pit. Mainly used for fixing prices when cash commodities are being brought.
Export Enhancement Program (EEP)	This US programme, established in early 1985, allows exporters to sell American products to foreign customers at world market prices: the United States Department of Agriculture subsidises the difference in the world price and the higher domestic price, which exporters have to pay for the product, in the form of commodities from the Commodity Credit Corporation inventory. The programme is targeted to countries benefiting from subsidised imports from non-US exporters. See **Commodity Credit Corporation (CCC)**.
Export Quota	(a) Quota set under an international commodity agreement whereby exporting countries of a particular commodity accept limits on their exports. (b) Bilateral or multilateral agreement between countries governing exports of industrial or other goods.
Export Refunds	Refunds or restitutions made under the EC's Common Agricultural Policy on exports of grain, beef, skimmed milk powder etc. The refunds are intended to help exports by offsetting the difference between the internal EC price and lower world price.
Ex Store	Term relating to the sale of commodities currently held in a warehouse or other storage facility.
Extraction Industry	Industry involved in extracting raw materials from the land, sea or air.
Extraction Rate	Proportion by weight of a processed product to its raw material.

Fabricator   Company which makes semi-fabricated products from refined metal and sometimes from scrap.

FAQ   Fair average quality. Used in the sale of agricultural commodities, i.e. average grade based on samples rather than on a specific grade.

Fats And Oils   Key products in international commodity and agricultural trade. They comprise animal fats and vegetable oils.

Feed Concentrates   Term covering corn (maize), sorghum, barley, oats, wheat, rye, oilseed meal, used in the production of animal feeds.

Feed Grains   Cereals used for animal fodder such as corn, sorghum, barley and oats as well as feed wheat, feed rye. See **Animal Feed Ingredients**.

Feed Ratios   Relationship between the cost of feeding animals and their market price expressed as a ratio.

Feeder Cattle   Young cattle that are ready to be fattened for slaughter.

FEFAC   Fédération Européenne des Fabricants d'Aliments Composés pour Animaux. The Brussels-based European Federation of Manufacturers of Animal Feed Compounds.

Financials   Market term referring to futures or options based on interest rates, currencies, stocks indices, bonds and equities often involving cash settlement.

Fine Grains   Wheat, rice. See **Coarse Grains**.

Fineness   Quality or purity of precious metals.

First Notice Day   First day on which sellers of commodities can inform purchasers, through the clearing house, of their intent to deliver actual commodities against futures contracts. See **Notice Day**.

Fishmeal   Fish processed into meal and used for livestock and poultry feed after extracting fish oil.

Fonds d'Intervention Et De Régularisation Du Marché Du Sucre (FIRS)   The French sugar market intervention board.

Food And Agriculture Organisation (FAO)   A United Nations organisation established to improve world agriculture, fishing and forestry. Based in Rome it also provides technical assistance, food aid and issues forecasts and statistics on the world agricultural outlook. See **World Food Programme**.

Food Balance Overall availability of food supplies compared with the population to be fed.

Force Majeure Occurrence outside the control of parties to a contract. A force majeure clause exempts the parties from their obligations under the contract if such an occurrence, e.g. an earthquake or typhoon, takes place. Companies often invoke such a clause if a serious labour dispute interrupts delivery of their goods.

FORMA Fonds d'Organisation et de Régularisation des Marchés Agricoles. French governmental organisation aimed at stabilising farm prices. It also acts as the intervention organisation in France for a number of products governed by EC agricultural policy rules.

Fortified Foods Foods to which vitamins, minerals, protein etc. have been added to improve their nutritional qualities.

Forward Contracting Cash transaction under which the buyer and seller agree on the delivery of a specified quality and quantity of a commodity or other goods at a specified future date. The price may be fixed beforehand or at delivery.

Forward Purchase/Sale Buying/selling of a physical commodity for receipt/delivery at a later date.

Forward Shipment Agreement for the shipment of cash commodities at a set future date.

Free Supply Commodity stocks available for sale, as opposed to government-owned or controlled stocks.

Fructose See Isoglucose.

Futures Standardised contracts for the purchase or sale of financial instruments or physical commodities for future delivery on a commodity exchange.

Futures Commission Merchant Individual or legal entity registered with the Commodity Futures Trading Commission in the USA who solicits business from others for execution on a listed commodity exchange.

Futures Market Organised exchange where standardised contracts for the future delivery of various commodities and financial instruments are traded according to established rules and regulations.

Gasohol See entry under ENERGY.

General Services Administration (GSA)
US government agency that buys and sells metals and other commodities for the US strategic stockpile.

Generic Commodity Certificates
Issued by the US Department of Agriculture, these are expressed in dollar value and can be redeemed for Commodity Credit Corporation commodities or in some cases, cash. They can also be sold for cash to other producers or commercial interests.

GEPLACEA
Grupo de Países Latinoamericano y del Caribe Exportadores de Azúcar. Formed in 1976, the Group of Latin American and Caribbean Sugar Exporting Countries acts as a forum for consultation on the production and sale of sugar. Its headquarters are in Mexico City.

Gold
Precious metal of which some 80 per cent of world production comes from South Africa and the Soviet Union. Jewellery accounts for about half the world consumption, while industrial uses make up less than 10 per cent.

Gold Certificates
(a) Document certifying the ownership of gold held at an authorised or recognised depository, mainly in the USA.
(b) In West Germany, banks sell certificates to residents which entitle the purchaser to ownership of gold deposited in Luxembourg, thereby allowing the purchaser to escape German value added tax on purchases of the metal.

Gold Fix
Routine twice daily fixing at 1030 and 1500 hours of the free market gold price by the five participating London bullion houses. The fix involves the matching of the bid and offer price.

Gold Loans
Loans whereby mining companies raise finance by borrowing gold to be repaid out of future production.

Good Delivery
Delivery of commodities or securities in good and due form; a delivery which meets contract conditions.

Grades
Standards set for judging the quality of a commodity.

Grain Reserve
US government-operated stockpile of grain designed to keep surplus supplies off the market until prices reach relatively high levels and allow for release of the grain.

Green Currency
Notional currency used when implementing EC Common Agricultural Policy rates, sometimes called Green Rates. The currencies of EC member states are fixed in terms of European units of account. These fixed values are known as green currencies, i.e. artificial exchange rates. Thus the value of a member state's currency in the sphere of

agricultural produce is fixed by administrative decision rather than by free market forces.

Gross Processing Margin (GPM) Difference between the cost of raw materials and the sales revenue from finished products.

Groundnuts Oilseed, also known as peanuts, used to produce vegetable oil and meal for animal feed, although also for human consumption. Grown mainly in tropical and sub-tropical regions.

Growths Type of coffee, cocoa, cotton etc. according to area or country in which it is produced.

Heavy Grains (HG) Wheat, maize and rye.

Hedge Establishment of a position on a commodity futures market which is equal and opposite to a transaction made on an actual or physical market. Hedging minimises the risk of inventory loss or locks in a profit due to price fluctuations by taking equal and opposite positions in cash and futures.

HFCS High fructose corn syrup. See **Isoglucose**.

Instituto Brasileiro De Café (IBC) Brazilian Coffee Institute. It sets parameters for Brazilian coffee export policy such as on quotas and pricing but actual sales are made through private companies.

Instituto do Açucar E Do Alcool (IAA) Brazilian Sugar and Alcohol Institute. It controls Brazilian sugar production and exports although current plans are to turn exports over to the private sector.

Integrated Producer A producer which owns mines, smelters and refineries and also, in some instances, fabricating plants.

Interafrican Coffee Organization (IACO) Producer group of African coffee countries which acts as a consultative and lobby body to the International Coffee Organization (ICO).

International Cocoa Organization (ICCO) Group of cocoa importing and exporting countries which participate in the International Cocoa Agreement (ICCA). It has attempted to stabilise prices by operating a buffer stock to buy when prices are weak and sell when they are strong. It also collects crop statistics.

International Coffee Organization (ICO) Group of coffee importing and exporting countries which participate in the International Coffee Agreement (ICA), a pact which aims to stabilise prices in a set range through operation of export quotas. It also collects crop statistics. **Non-ICO Market**—Parallel market outside ICA rules at prices which are often lower than the official market.

International Commodities Clearing House (ICCH)	Owned by major British banks, the ICCH clears and guarantees trades in financial futures and commodity markets in London and in several overseas centres including Australia, New Zealand, Hong Kong and Paris.
International Lead And Zinc Study Group (ILZSG)	Brings together producing/consuming countries and industry representatives. It collects statistics, but has no market regulatory functions.
International Natural Rubber Organization (INRO)	Group of producing and consuming countries which participate in the International Natural Rubber Agreement (INRA), a pact which seeks to stabilise prices through the operation of a buffer stock.
International Rubber Study Group (IRSG)	Intergovernmental organisation mainly representing synthetic and natural rubber producers. It collects statistics, carries out economic studies and provides a forum to discuss matters affecting supply and demand of rubber.
International Sugar Organization (ISO)	Group of sugar importing and exporting countries which have formed the International Sugar Agreement (ISA). The current pact is administrative and has no working market regulatory or economic clauses.
International Tin Council (ITC)	Organisation grouping tin consumer and producer nations which previously regulated the tin market through its buffer stock under the International Tin Agreement (ITA) until it ran out of funds in October 1985. The ITC is now involved in lengthy legal actions with creditors and is due to be replaced, as far as statistical studies are involved, by an International Tin Study Group (ITSG). Assets of the ITC were frozen in July 1988.
International Wheat Council (IWC)	Group of wheat producing and consuming countries which cooperate under the International Wheat Agreement (IWA). The agreement has no market regulatory or economic clauses but provides for the collection of statistics on world wheat and coarse grain production.
International Wrought Copper Council (IWCC)	Industry group consisting of European, Japanese and Australian consumers which keeps statistics on the world copper market.
Intervention	See entry under ECONOMY, CURRENCY.
Inverted Market	Commodities futures market where the price of near months is higher than deferred months, i.e. prices are inverted. Such a price structure normally reflects a shortage of supplies. See **Backwardation**.
Isoglucose	Isoglucose or, as it is known in the USA, high fructose corn

syrup (HFCS), is a sweetener derived from corn/maize and used in soft drinks and manufactured products. Increasingly displacing sugar in industry but not yet for household use.

Invisible Supply   Stocks (especially commodities) outside commercial channels whose exact quantity cannot be identified but which in theory are available to the market.

Job Lot   Unit of trading smaller or larger than the regular contract unit.

Jute   Plant fibre used for sacking, mats, cord.

Large Trader   Trader who holds or controls a position in any one future of a commodity on any one contract market equal to or greater than the reporting level.

Last Trading Day   Last day for trading a futures contract in the current delivery month. Positions which have not been closed by this date must be fulfilled by making or taking delivery of the physical commodity.

Latex   Found in the milky white fluid produced by rubber trees, which is in the form of 30 per cent latex and 70 per cent water. See **Rubber**.

Laurics   Oilseed marked term for palm seed and coconut products.

Lead   Base metal mainly used in storage batteries. The USA, Canada, Peru, Australia and the Soviet Union are major producers.

Légumes   Plants such as soybeans which produce pods containing seeds that are eaten or crushed. They also help nitrogen enrichment of the soil.

Lending   London Metal Exchange term for the sale of a nearby delivery date coupled with the simultaneous purchase of a more distant date. See **Borrowing**.

Licensed Warehouse   Warehouse approved by an exchange from which a commodity may be delivered under a futures contract.

Light Grains   Barley and oats.

Limit Up/Down   Maximum price fluctuation permitted in certain commodities or securities markets within any one session. The maximum advance and decline from the previous day's settlement price permitted in one trading session are known as limit up and limit down. Some markets do not trade again during the session after a limit move unless prices fall (or rise), while others suspend trading temporarily upon hitting limit levels and then re-open with expanded limits. See **Minimum/ Maximum Price Fluctuation**. See **Price Limit** and **Trading Limit** under GENERAL MARKET TERMS.

Linseed
Variety of flaxseed used to produce linseed oil/linoil and protein meal for animal feed. Linoil is used in paints/ varnishes and also in linoleum.

Liquidation
Closing of a long or short futures position by concluding a covering sales or purchase.

Loan Rate
The price per unit (such as bushel, bale or pound weight) at which the US government makes loans to farmers, enabling them to hold their crops for later sale. The loan rate has served as a floor to the market because farmers can default if the market falls below the loan rate, forfeiting their grain to the Commodity Credit Corporation rather than paying back the loan and selling on the open market. See **Commodity Credit Corporation (CCC)** and **Marketing Loan**.

Loco
Cost of goods where they lie, or including packing and delivery at the place named in the price quotation.

Lodging
Describes the condition of grain crops when bent over and broken (e.g. by wind or rain), making the crop difficult to harvest.

Lomé Convention
Agreement between the EC and a number of developing countries in Africa, the Caribbean and the Pacific. Covers trade preferences and development assistance. See **ACP States**.

London FOX
London Futures and Options Exchange. New name for the London Commodity Exchange (LCE) which is the parent company of UK cocoa, coffee and sugar futures markets. It also provides trading facilities for the International Petroleum Exchange (IPE). See **International Petroleum Exchange (IPE)** under ENERGY.

Long Hedge
Buying of futures contracts in expectation of actual cash market purchases.

Long Ton
Ton of 2,240 lbs, equal to 1.016 tonnes.

Lot
The unit of trading especially in commodities. More or less than the standard unit is described as an odd or job lot.

Maize
European term interchangeable with US corn. See **Corn**.

Management Committees (EC)
Groups run by the EC Commission, comprising experts from national ministries overseeing the working of EC policies, e.g. for dairy products, sugar and cereals. EC national

governments enjoy limited powers within these committees to block Commission decisions.

Manmade Fibres
Industrially produced fibres as opposed to natural fibres such as cotton and wool. Includes both artificial and synthetic fibres.

Margin
In commodities it is the amount of money or collateral deposited with a broker, or with a clearing house, to insure against loss on open futures contracts. It is not a part payment on a purchase. Maintenance margin is the amount which must be maintained on deposit with the broker at all times. See entry under EQUITIES.

Margin Call
If a commodity futures or securities market moves against a trade or speculator, he may receive a margin call to provide extra finance or security to maintain his margin.

Market Order
An order to buy or sell futures contracts that is to be filled as soon as possible at the competitive market price.

Marketing Loan
Scheme where US crop loan can be repaid at the world market price instead of the original loan rate if the world price is lower. Congress authorised its use for grains, oilseeds and cotton in the 1985 farm bill to permit US prices in export markets to fall below loan rate levels, but in 1988 it had only been implemented for rice and cotton. See **Loan Rate**.

Marketing Year
Period during which a commodity (usually agricultural) is sold. Generally starts with the harvest. See **Crop Year**.

Maturity
The period within which a futures contract can be settled by the delivery of the actual commodity. Maturity date is the delivery or settlement date for a futures contract. See entry under LENDING.

Maximum/ Minimum Price Fluctuation
According to the rules of a commodity exchange, this is the maximum or minimum movement allowed in the price of a futures contract in all or part of a trading session. See **Limit Up/Down**.

Metric Ton (Tonne)
2,204.6223 lbs, or 1,000 kilos.

Milo
US term for grain sorghum.

MIT
Market if touched. A commodity order to sell or buy at a specific price, if the market reaches that price.

Molasses
Syrup remaining after the sugar separated by crystallisation is removed during sugar refining. Also extracted from sorghum.

Monetary Compensatory Amount (MCA)	Border adjustment used to even out the differences between green currencies and the actual foreign exchange value of EC currencies. It is calculated weekly. The MCA acts as a subsidy on food imports for a country with a weak currency, since it brings prices down from the high green currency level to the lower foreign exchange or real value. By the same token, it makes farm exports from such countries dearer. For countries with strong currencies, exports are cheaper and imports dearer but it also ensures prices paid to farmers in those countries do not fall. See **Green Currency**.
Multi-Fibre Arrangement (MFA)	The arrangement, concluded in 1973 by some 50 countries meeting under the auspices of the General Agreement on Tariffs and Trade (GATT) in Geneva, lays down rules for international trade in textile products of wool, cotton and man-made fibres.
Nearbys	Nearest delivery months of a commodity futures contract. See **Deferred Futures**.
New Crop	Crop about to be, or having just been, harvested.
New York Cotton Exchange (NYCE)	Trades futures in cotton and frozen concentrated orange juice (FCOJ) contracts.
Nickel	Base metal mainly used in steel alloying. Main producers include Canada, the Soviet Union, the Philippines, Australia, New Caledonia, Cuba, Dominican Republic and Indonesia.
Notice Day	Day on which notices of intent to deliver on futures contracts may be issued.
NYMEX	New York Mercantile Exchange—Trades platinum and palladium futures in addition to energy futures. See entry under ENERGY.
Oats	High protein grain which can withstand cooler climates and poor soils. Used for animal feed and human consumption.
Odd Lot	Trading lot in a quantity or amount smaller or larger than the regular market lot.
Office National Interprofessionel Des Céréales (ONIC)	The French National Cereals Office.
Oilseed	Agricultural product from which vegetable oils and meals are extracted, e.g. soybeans.
Old Crop	Product from a previous harvest.

Olein　　A form of processed palm oil.

Open Position (Open Interest)　　Total of futures contracts open at any one time which have not yet been matched and closed by a corresponding opposite transaction, i.e. there has been no subsequent sale or purchase, nor has delivery been made or taken of the physical commodity or financial instrument. The extent of open interest provides a clue for the analyst as to the technical condition of the market. Also called Open Contracts or Open Commitments.

Origins　　Producing countries. "Origin sales" is a phrase often used to describe selling by a state marketing board or an exporter from a commodity-producing country.

Other Milds　　See **Coffee**.

Paddy　　Also Padi. Rough or harvested rice which has not been husked or processed.

Palm Kernel Oil　　Vegetable oil obtained from the kernel of the oil palm nut. Used in chemicals, confectionery, ice cream, cosmetics, margarine.

Palmoil　　Second to soyoil in world vegetable oil production. Produced from the pulp of the fruit (nut) of oil palms grown in tropical countries and sets as a soft solid at room temperature. Used for soap making and industrial purposes and, when refined, for margarine, edible oils etc.

Payment In Kind (PIK)　　As part of the US 1982/83 acreage reduction plan, grain farmers, who took land out of production, received as payment grains from Commodity Credit Corp (CCC) stocks rather than cash. In later years, PIK has referred to CCC Generic Certificates (called PIK certs by the trade), which farmers receive for participating in government programmes. These certificates are redeemable for a fixed dollar value of CCC stocks of any commodity, regardless of what the farmer would have planted. The value of redeemable commodities is set daily by the government. A secondary cash market has developed in the certificates. See **Commodity Credit Corporation**.

Physicals　　Actual commodities as opposed to futures contracts. See **Actuals**.

PIK And Roll　　A marketing strategy using commodity certificates, under which a US farmer puts his commodity under loan, collects the county loan level, purchases certificates equal to the value of the commodity just put under loan, then uses the certificates to redeem the commodity. The farmer obtains his profit by netting the difference between the high county loan rate and the lower certificate price.

Pit	Area on a trading floor where futures contract trading takes place. Also called a ring.
Platinum	Precious metal which for industrial purposes is mainly used as a catalyst in petrochemical output and pollution control systems, e.g. catalytic converters for car exhausts. South Africa and the USSR account for over 80 per cent of world production.
Polarisation	Measurement in degrees to define purity of sugar.
Pork Bellies	Part of a hog carcass which is processed into bacon.
Position Limit	Maximum position, either net long or net short, in one commodity futures or all futures of a single commodity which may be held or controlled by a single person under CFTC or exchange rules. Has a similar meaning with regard to listed options.
Position Trader	Someone who trades in the commodity futures market and maintains a long or short position for more than one trading session, as distinguished from a day trader who initiates and liquidates a futures position in the same trading session.
Pressure Burst	Sudden bursting of rock due to great pressure in deep mining.
Primary Commodities	Commodities in the raw or unprocessed state, e.g. iron ore.
Primary Metals	Metals produced from ores. See **Secondary Metals**.
Prompt Date	The date on which a commodity must be delivered to fulfil a contract.
Protection/Push Bids	Amendments made by US cash grain buyers to their daily posted basis bids to compensate for expected extreme movements in futures prices when the market opens. A buyer will take protection if futures are expected to open lower or push bids if the market is likely to open higher.
Public Elevators	Grain elevators in the USA used for the bulk storage of grains. Some elevators are approved delivery points for grain under futures contracts.
Public Law 480 (PL480)	Also known as the food for peace programme. The main US legislative authority for providing food and farm product aid to developing countries, in the form of outright donation or on long term credit at low interest. Enacted in 1954 as the Agricultural Trade Development and Assistance Act.
Pulses	Edible beans, lentils and peas.

Quintal

Unit of weight equal to 100 kilos.

Rapeseed

Major oilseed crop which yields a higher percentage of its weight in oil (as opposed to meal) than soybeans. Rapeseed is known in Canada as canola and in Europe as colza. Rapeoil is a general purpose edible vegetable oil, while meal is used as a protein foodstuff.

Raw Value

Unrefined sugar traditionally of 96 degrees polarity. See **Polarisation, White Value.**

Red Gold

Alloy consisting (for example) of 750 parts gold and 250 parts copper; copper can also produce a yellow alloy (as in 750 parts gold, 125 parts silver, 125 parts copper), yellower than gold itself.

Reef

Lode of gold-bearing quartz.

Registered Commodity Representative

Person in the USA who is registered with the Commodity Futures Trading Commission and the exchanges as seeking commodity business for his firm.

Regular Warehouse

Warehouse or storage facility approved as the point from which delivery, to fulfil a commodity futures contract, may take place.

Regularity

In the USA a processing plant, warehouse, mill, vault or bank that satisfies exchange requirements for financing, handling capacity and location, and which has been approved as acceptable for delivery of commodities against futures contracts.

Regulated Commodities

US futures markets in all commodities regulated since April 1975 under the Commodity Exchange Act as amended by the Commodity Futures Trading Act of 1974.

Reporting Limit

Size of positions in a market at or above which daily details are required by commodity, delivery month and whether it is a hedging or speculative position.

Rice

Important cereal grain. Unprocessed but harvested rice is known as "rough" or "paddy". Once the husk is removed it becomes "brown" or "cargo". When the husk and outer bran layers have been removed it becomes "milled" or "polished" rice.

Ring

Designated area used for trading at, for example, the London Metal Exchange.

Ring-Out

Method of settlement in 1986 of outstanding London Metal Exchange tin contracts after the collapse of the International Tin Council market support operations in 1985. The LME settled outstanding contracts at a price between the contract price and the prevailing market value, but no delivery took place.

Robusta   See **Arabica/Robusta**.

Round Turn   Completed commodity futures transaction through an initial purchase and subsequent sale (or vice versa) of the same month, offsetting each other on the same market.

RSS   Ribbed, Smoked Sheet. A type of rubber.

Rubber   Malaysia, Indonesia and Thailand are major producers of natural rubber, derived from Latex. The use of oil-based synthetic rubber, which accounts for 67–68 per cent of the total market, has been rising, but many industries still rely heavily on natural rubber.

Running Bales   Term used in the cotton trade to designate the number of bales of cotton as they come from the gin in varying weights.

Rust   Plant disease caused by fungi, which reduces yields, e.g. coffee rust.

Rye   Widely grown cereal used for dark bread, alcohol and livestock feed. It is able to withstand cooler temperatures and poorer soils.

Sample Grade   Usually the lowest quality of commodity acceptable for delivery under a futures contract.

Secondary Market In commodities, sale or resale by an intermediary rather than a first-hand seller. Also called secondhand market. See entry under LENDING.

Secondary Metals Product of refining scrap or alloys as opposed to primary metals produced from ore. See **Primary Metals**.

Set-Aside   Leaving land idle, letting land lie fallow. Part of US and European Community policies to curb farm surpluses by encouraging farmers to take land out of agricultural production.

Settlement Price Average price at the close of the day's trading in commodities, usually used to set the next day's fluctuation limits and to determine margin calls on futures contracts.

Short Ton   Ton of 2,000 lbs or 0.907 tonne.

Silo   (a) Pit or airtight structure in which green crops are pressed and kept for fodder, undergoing fermentation. (b) Pit or tower to store grain.

Silver

Precious metal used industrially due to its excellent heat and electricity conducting properties. Major producers include Mexico, Peru, the Soviet Union, Canada, Australia and the USA.

SIR

Standard Indonesian Rubber.

Sisal

Plant that produces fibre used for ropes and cords.

Sorghum

Grain grown in warmer climates which competes with corn and is largely used for animal feed. It is also called milo in the USA.

Soybean

The dominant world oilseed, making up 50 per cent or more of total world oilseed production. It is crushed into meal, the major use of which is in animal feed, and oil used for salad oil, margarine, etc.

Special Committee On Agriculture (EC)

EC committee grouping the top agricultural experts in each of the national permanent delegations to the EC with national governmental and Commission representatives. Its task is to try to establish what is politically feasible in the EC agricultural sector.

Spread

Gap in a quotation between buying and selling prices, e.g. the difference between the purchase of one futures delivery month against the sale of another delivery month of the same commodity. See entry under LENDING.

Squeeze

Pressures exerted on one commodity's delivery, usually spot, when the price is exaggerated (upwards) against the rest of the market. See entry under ECONOMY, CURRENCY.

Stabex

EC programme for helping developing countries under the Lomé Convention by stabilising export commodity earnings, i.e. by providing EC subsidies for those countries in the scheme whose earnings fall below a certain level.

Stabiliser/ Budgetary Stabiliser

European Community mechanisms under which farm support prices are cut and/or co-responsibility levies increased if EC production exceeds a fixed ceiling. See **Co-Responsibility Levy**.

Stope

A place to extract ore inside a mine.

Sugar Beet

The most important source of sugar in temperate countries. The crop is harvested in the autumn and early winter. The European Community and the Soviet Union are the biggest beet producers.

Sugar Cane   Provides more than half the world's supply of sugar. The crop is planted by stem cuttings and the first harvest is ready about a year later. After cutting, the plants grow successive crops of stems which take about the same period to mature. Main cane producers are Brazil, Cuba, India and Mexico.

Sunflower/ Sunflowerseed   A major oilseed crop yielding more oil and less meal than soybeans per unit weight of oilseed.

Supplmentary Levy (EC)   Additional levy charged on imports of certain farm products under the EC's Common Agricultural Policy.

Switching   Also called "rolling forward". See entry under GENERAL MARKET TERMS.

Tael   See **Troy Ounce**.

Target Price   In the USA, a price level established by law for wheat, feedgrains, rice and cotton. If the market price falls below the target price, an amount equal to the difference (but not more than the difference between the target price and price-support loan levels) is paid to farmers who participate in commodity programmes. In the European Community, the target price is fixed by the authorities as the desirable wholesale price for grain delivered to the area of greatest deficit in the Community. See **Deficiency Payments** and **Loan Rate**.

Tel Quel   Weight of sugar in metric or long tons, given without regard to whether it is in white, raw or crystal form.

Tender   (a) Notice of intent to deliver physical goods against a commodity futures contract. (b) An invitation to acquire or sell a physical product. In a "buy tender" a country sets out the terms under which it will purchase sugar, grain etc; in a "sell tender" it states that it wishes to sell e.g. a specific quantity of a crop for delivery at a specified time.

Tenderable Grades   Also called deliverable grades, these refer to grades and staples designated as deliverable to settle a futures contract.

Terminal Market   Commodity market where physicals are exchanged for cash and are deliverable against maturing futures contracts.

Threshold Price   In the European Community, minimum price at which grain from a non-member state can enter the EC market. Import levies are imposed to bridge the gap between (normally) lower world prices and the threshold price. The aim is to prevent low-priced grain from outside the EC disrupting the EC market.

Tin	Base metal largely used in tinplate production for the canning industry. Tin is facing increasing competition from aluminium. Main producing countries are Malaysia, Thailand, Indonesia, Brazil, China, Bolivia and Australia.
Tokyo Commodity Exchange For Industry (TOCOM)	Trades gold, silver, platinum, rubber, cotton yarn contracts.
Ton/Tonne	See **Metric Ton**, **Long Ton** and **Short Ton**.
Trigger Price	The price level at which buy/sell mechanisms, provided for in commodity agreements, take effect.
Triple Nine	Highest degree of gold purity or 99.9 per cent pure gold.
Troy Ounce	The traditional unit of weight for gold in the Anglo-Saxon system of weights and measures. 1 oz troy equals a rounded 31.1035 grammes. In the Middle East and on the Indian subcontinent the traditional unit of measure is the tola, equal to 11.6638g or 0.375 oz. In the Far East, on the other hand, gold is traded in taels (1 tael equals 37.4290g or 1.20337 oz).
US Department Of Agriculture (USDA)	US government department responsible for implementing agricultural policy. It is also a major source of forecasts and statistics on agriculture in the USA and worldwide. See **ASCS** and **Commodity Credit Corporation**.
Warrant	Document of title to metal stored in a London Metal Exchange-listed warehouse. See entry under LENDING.
Warehouse Receipt	Document providing proof of ownership of a specified quality and quantity of a commodity at a designated warehouse.
Wheat	A major export grain in world trade. Main US export categories consist of Hard Red Winter, Hard Red Spring, Durum, White and Soft Red Winter. Winter wheat is planted in the autumn and harvested in the late spring and summer of the following year. Spring wheat is planted in the spring and harvested the same year.
White Gold	Alloy consisting (for example) of 750 parts gold, 150 parts nickel and 100 parts copper. The copper-nickel portion can be replaced by platinum or palladium.
White Value	Refers to refined sugar of 99.9 polarisation.
Winter Kill	Damage caused to a crop by cold winter weather.
Wintering	The period when rubber trees shed leaves and production declines.

Winze   In mining, excavation of a reef made downards to connect
                         drives on different levels.

World Food   Multilateral food aid organisation set up by the Food and
Programme   Agriculture Organisation and the United Nations in 1962 to
                         help less developed countries and deal with food
                         emergencies.

Energy

Accommodation Platform/Rig
Platform or semi-submersible rig built or adapted to act as a "hotel" for offshore personnel.

Acidization
Process whereby acid is injected into reservoir rock, thereby enlarging the pore spaces and increasing the flow of oil.

AFRA
See entry under SHIPPING.

Allocation
Planned sharing of crude oil or petroleum products: either voluntary, adopted by a supplier, or mandatory, imposed by government.

American Petroleum Institute (API)
A US industry trade group that has established standards and measurements for the drilling, refining and petrochemical industries. The API publishes an important weekly report on US petroleum inventories, imports and refinery utilisation.

Anhydrous Ammonia
"Dry" ammonia, i.e. containing no dissolved water. It is one of the most important petroleum-derived raw materials used in the chemical industry.

API Gravity
Universally accepted scale adopted by the American Petroleum Institute for expressing the specific gravity of oils:

$$\text{API gravity} = \frac{141.5}{\text{specific gravity at 60 degs F}} - 131.5$$

API gravity serves as a rough measure of quality—the higher the API gravity number, the richer the yield in premium refined products. Saudi Arabian Light has an API gravity of 34, whilst Algerian Saharan has an API gravity of 44.

Appraisal Drilling
Drilling carried out to determine the physical extent, reserves and likely production rate of an oil or gas field.

Aromatics
A group of hydrocarbon fractions that can be transformed into numerous chemicals. Benzene, toluene and xylene are the principal aromatics.

Asphalt
A solid hydrocarbon found as a natural deposit. Crude oil with a high asphalt content that is refined to remove the lighter fractions such as naphtha and kerosene leaves asphalt as a residue.

Associated Gas
Natural gas found in association with oil, either dissolved in the oil or as a cap of free gas above the oil.

Associated Liquids Liquid hydrocarbons found in association with natural gas.

ASTM American Society for Testing Materials. Responsible for issuing many of the standard methods used in the oil industry.

Avails The quantities of crude that oil firms expect to be available from foreign fields in a particular period or year.

Aviation Turbine Kerosene (ATK) Medium-light fuel burned in jet and turbo-prop aircraft engines.

Barge Non self-propelled vessel used as a base for drilling equipment, to carry cranes, support facilities, accommodation modules etc, to lay underwater pipelines or to transport crude oil or its products over short distances such as on rivers or lakes.

Barrels Volume measurement of liquid in the petroleum industry, equal to 42 US gallons or 36 Imperial gallons, or about 0.136 tonnes depending upon specific gravity ranging from 7.1 to 7.8 barrels per tonne.

Barrels Per Day (BPD) Represents the total volume of oil produced from a field, carried through a pipeline, or processed, divided by number of days in the period. One barrel per day is equivalent to around 50 tonnes per annum, depending upon specific gravity.

Basic Petrochemical Basic raw material manufactured from crude oil by steam cracking or reforming, e.g. ethylene, benzene.

Batching Sequence The order in which product shipments are sent through a pipeline.

Bed Layer of sediments or sedimentary rock of considerable thickness and uniform composition and texture.

Benzene Key petroleum-derived raw material used in the chemical industry.

Bit See **Drill Bit**.

Blowout When gas, oil or salt water, usually by accident, escapes from a well due to release of pressure in the reservoir rock not controlled by the containment systems, or to failure of the containment systems during production.

Blowout Preventor (BOP) Hydraulically-operated safety valve which automatically closes a well if the drill bit hits high pressure hydrocarbons.

Boiling Range   Distillation range.

British Thermal Unit (BTU)   Heat needed to raise one pound of air-free water from 60 degrees Fahrenheit to 61 degrees at a constant pressure of one atmosphere.

Bunker 'C'   Heavy residual fuel oil used by ships, industry and for large scale heating installations.

Bunker Fuel   Any fuel oil or diesel fuel used by ships.

Butane   See **Liquefied Petroleum Gas (LPG)**.

Buyback Price   Purchase price an oil company pays to a country for oil that the company produces but which belongs to that country.

Carbon Black   Substantially pure form of finely divided carbon based on liquid or gaseous hydrocarbons, used in making rubber products and inks.

Carried Interest   When a company pays for all or part of a partner's costs during exploration or development, e.g. when a company "carries" a state that retains a participation interest in the field.

Casing   The steel lining which supports the sides of the well and prevents water or gas from entering.

Catalyst   Substance aiding or promoting a chemical reaction but remaining chemically unchanged after the reaction.

Catalytic Cracking   The process whereby heavy hydrocarbon molecules are broken down (cracked) into lighter molecules by passing them over a suitable catalyst (generally heated).

Choke   Heavy steel valve used to restrict the size of the opening through which oil or gas flows, thus controlling production.

Christmas Tree   Assembly of pipes and valves attached to a production wellhead controlling the flow of oil or gas and stopping a possible blowout.

Clean (White)   Highly refined oil products, such as aviation spirit, motor spirit, kerosene and some grades of gas oil.

Coal Equivalent   Used in energy consumption statistics as an overall measure.

Coal Gasification   A process for producing natural gas by heating coal.

Coal (Hydrogenated)   Production of artificial mineral oil from coal by combining the carbon in coal with hydrogen to form hydrocarbon.

Commercial Field Oil and/or gas field able to generate sufficient income to make it worth developing.

Completion The process by which a finished well is either sealed off or prepared for production by fitting a wellhead.

Concession A licence area leased to a company for a given period for exploration and development, usually specifying the area to be explored, how long the concession will last and how the area's owner (i.e. a government) is to be compensated if oil or gas is found.

Condensates A mixture of hydrocarbons which occur as vapour in underground gas reservoirs and condense to liquids when brought to the surface.

Condenser Equipment which changes a material from a vapour to a liquid state.

Conservation Regulation of oil or gas production from a reservoir in order to prolong its life and recover a larger quantity of the oil or gas in place.

Continental Shelf Edge of a continental mass, of varying width, that lies under the sea in comparatively shallow water (up to 200 metres depth).

Core Cylindrical rock sample cut from the well during drilling by means of an annular cutter.

Crack Spread A calculation showing the theoretical market value of petroleum products that could be derived from a barrel of crude after the oil is refined or cracked. The crack spread does not represent the refining margin because a barrel of crude yields a varying amount of petroleum products such as heating oil, gasoline, jet fuel and kerosene.

Cracking Production process in the petroleum industry whereby feedstock is subjected to a high temperature for a limited period in order to boost the output of light products at the expense of heavier types of fuel. See **Catalytic Cracking** and **Thermal Cracking**.

Crude Oil Oil produced from a reservoir after any associated gas has been removed.

Crude Participation Oil belonging to the host government in proportion to its stake in the company. Mainly sold for distribution by the companies at a buyback price. See **Buyback Price**.

Cubic Participation The standard unit of measurement for quantities of gas at atmospheric pressure. 1 cu.ft. = 0.0283 cubic metres.

Dedicated Reserves	Natural gas reserves committed by the owner to a specific buyer under a long-term contract.
Depletion Control	Restriction on the rate at which oil and gas and other mineral reserves can be used.
Derived Fuel	Form of energy manufactured from a primary fuel such as coal or oil, e.g. electricity, coke or town gas.
DERV	Diesel Engine Road Vehicle fuel derived from gas oil (UK term).
Detergent	Cleansing liquid or solid, normally made from petroleum products.
Development Phase	Period when a proven oil or gas field is brought into production by drilling production wells.
Development Well	Well used to produce oil or gas from a proven field.
Deviated Well	Well drilled at an angle rather than vertically, primarily to allow as large an area as possible to be drained of hydrocarbons from a single production platform.
Diesel Fuel	Light oil fuel used in diesel engines.
Dirty (Black)	Crude oils, fuel oil and some lower grades of gas oil.
Discovery Well	Exploratory well that finds new reserves of oil or gas.
Distillates	Products resulting from condensation during distillation in a refinery, i.e. gaseous fuels, gas oil and kerosene oils.
Distillation	Refining process which separates or purifies liquids by successive vaporisation and condensation.
Downstream	Refers to operations that take place after crude is produced such as refining, transportaion and marketing.
Drill Bit	Head of a drilling tool which cuts through rock.
Drill Collars	Heavy steel tubing located immediately above the drill bit to maintain pressure on the bit and keep the drill string in tension.
Drill Ship	Vessel with a derrick for drilling in waters which are too deep for a jack-up or semi-submersible rig.
Drill Stem Test (DST)	Test of the formation fluids in a possible oil or gas bearing stratum by letting them flow to the surface through the drill

string under carefully controlled conditions.

Drill String   Steel piping in approximately 10 metre lengths connecting the bit to the drilling rig. As it rotates, it drills the hole and permits the lubricating mud to circulate. Sometimes called the drill pipe.

Drilling Mud   Mix of clays, water and chemicals pumped down the drill string to lubricate the system, while carrying away rock cuttings, maintaining pressure at the bit end.

Drilling Platform   Platform for drilling offshore exploration and development wells but without the processing facilities found on a production platform.

Drilling Rig   A mobile apparatus carrying all the equipment needed for drilling a well. See **Drill Ship, Jack-Up Rig, Semi-Submersible Rig** and **Drilling Platform.**

Dry Hole   Non-productive well, i.e. no gas or oil in commercial quantities.

Dry Natural Gas   Natural gas with few associated liquids, mostly methane.

Equity Crude   A company's share of oil production in a concession, normally given in proportion to its stake in the field.

Ethane   Colourless, odourless gas, sometimes extracted from natural gas as feedstock for the chemical industry.

Exchanges   Trades of crude or products between producers or refiners, usually done for quality reasons or to save transportation costs.

Exploration Drilling   Drilling carried out to establish whether hydrocarbons are present in a particular area or structure.

Farm In   This describes what happens when one company acquires an interest in an exploration or production licence by paying some of the past or future costs of another company which is relinquishing part of its interest.

Farm Out   A company relinquishes part of its interest in an exploration or production licence to another company in return for part-payment of its costs.

Federal Energy Regulatory Commission (FERC)   An agency within the US Department of Energy that oversees regulation of interstate natural gas pipelines and gas prices.

Feedstock	Provision of crude oil, natural gas liquids or natural gas to a refinery or petrochemical plant, or the supply of an intermediate petrochemical. (Crude oil is the raw material processed at a refinery, naphtha at an ethylene plant etc.)
Flaring	Burning off gas resulting from oil extraction which cannot be stored, reinjected or shipped ashore.
Flash Point	Lowest temperature at which vapour from oil will ignite when briefly exposed to a source of ignition.
Flotel	Floating accommodation rig or barge used as quarters for offshore personnel.
Fractions	Liquid hydrocarbons with a given boiling range, produced during the fractional distillation process.
Fractional Column	Tall tower in which fractional distillation takes place and which produces different distillates.
Fractional Distillation	Separation of crude oil or one of its components into liquids of different boiling ranges (fractions) by distillation; the basic process occurring in an oil refinery.
Fuel Oil	Heavy distillates from the oil refining process; used as fuel for power stations, industry, and marine boilers.
Gas Cap	Layer of natural gas above the oil in an oil reservoir.
Gas Injection	Process of pumping separated associated gas back into a reservoir for conservation purposes or to maintain the reservoir pressure.
Gas Oil	Petroleum distillates from the oil refining process, intermediate between light and lubricating oils and kerosene. Used to produce diesel fuel and for burning in certain central heating systems. Known as heating oil in the USA. See **Home Heating Oil**.
Gas to Oil Ratio	Number of cubic feet of gas per barrel of oil at atmospheric pressure, or as the volume of gas to volume of oil.
Gasification	Manufacture of gaseous fuel from a solid or liquid fuel.
Gasohol	Mixture usually of 90 parts unleaded gasoline and 10 parts ethanol, often distilled from grain or sugar cane.
Gasoline	Light petroleum distillate used in spark-ignited petroleum combustion engines. Equivalent to motor spirit or petrol.
Gusher	Flowing well, possibly not under control.

Heavy Crude Oil	Thick, viscous crudes with a high specific gravity but a low API gravity (of 20 degrees or less). Extraction of heavy crudes requires special costly techniques such as steam injection. See **API Gravity**.
Home Heating Oil	A light gas oil that is similar to diesel fuel, often used for domestic heating. The most widely used type is No. 2 heating oil. See **Gas Oil**.
Hydrocarbons	Materials composed of hydrogen and carbon. They may be found as solids, liquids or gas.
Hydrocracking	Refining technique for converting residual petroleum liquids into high octane gasoline, jet fuels and fuel oils.
Hyperbaric Chamber	Chamber with a high internal pressure allowing divers to live under the same pressure conditions at which they work under water. A chamber in which divers work or are transported under water. See **Saturation Diving**.
Independent	The term generally applies to a non-integrated oil company, usually active in only one or two sectors of the industry. An independent marketer buys product from major or independent refiners and resells it under its own brand name. There are also independents which are active either in refining or crude production exclusively.
Infill Drilling	The development of an oil or gas field by drilling additional wells between existing wells.
Integrated Oil Company	A firm that performs all the principal oil industry functions— exploration, production, transportation, refining and marketing. See **Majors**.
International Energy Agency (IEA)	Formed after the 1973 oil crisis by the 21 leading Western oil consuming nations to prevent another oil crisis. Headquartered in Paris.
International Petroleum Exchange (IPE)	Market in London which trades gas oil, crude, gasoline and heavy fuel oil futures.
Injection Well	Used to inject gas or water into the reservoir to maintain pressure during secondary recovery for conservation purposes.
IP	Institute of Petroleum. The official British organisation which deals with petroleum technology and with the standardisation of test methods for petroleum.
Isopach Map	Geological map giving the thickness of a particular stratum.

Jacket Platform   Platform constructed entirely of steel and normally kept in position by steel piles driven into the sea bed.

Jack-Up Rig   Mobile offshore drilling platform with retractable legs on which the platform rests on the sea bed when in use.

Jet Fuel   See **Kerosene**.

Junked   When equipment is lost down a well and cannot be retrieved economically, the well is junked, i.e. plugged and abandoned.

Jurassic Era   Period in geological time which began roughly 180 million years ago and ended roughly 130 million years ago. See **Palaeozoic** and **Triassic**.

Kelly   Square or hexagonal hollow pipe which engages at one end with a drilling table and at the other with a drill pipe.

Kerosene   Medium-light distillate, used for lighting and heating, and to provide fuel for jet and turbo-prop aircraft engines; also spelt kerosine. In the UK called paraffin or paraffin oil.

Killing A Well   Overcoming the tendency of a well to flow naturally by filling the well bore with drilling mud or a similar substance.

Landed Price   Total cost of oil to a refiner, after accounting for all costs from site of production or purchase to the refinery.

Landman   Oil company executive primarily concerned with securing oil and gas leases.

Lay Barge   Barge built for laying submarine pipelines.

Licence Block   Continental Shelf section in a particular national sector bounded by latitude and longitude lines, usually at one-degree intervals. It is usually sub-divided further into smaller quantities than a company contracted for.

Lifting   Oil companies "lift" crude or products when their tankers or barges take on cargoes at export terminals or trans-shipment points: "underlifting" means to load smaller quantities than a company contracted for.

Light Crude   Low specific gravity crude with high API gravity.

Light Ends   The more volatile products of petroleum refining, e.g. butane, propane, gasoline.

Liquefied Natural Gas (LNG)   Natural gas that has been liquefied by refrigeration or pressure in order to facilitate storage or transport; generally consists mainly of methane.

Liquefied Petroleum Gas (LPG) Light hydrocarbons from oil-bearing strata which are gaseous at normal temperatures but which are liquefied by refrigeration or pressure to facilitate storage or transport. Mainly propane and butane.

Log See **Well Logging**.

LOOP An abbreviation for Louisiana Offshore Oil Port which is the only US deepwater port able to offload huge tankers. LOOP is located in the Gulf of Mexico near New Orleans, and can offload up to 1.4 million barrels a day.

Lubricant Substance, generally based on heavy liquid hydrocarbons, used to reduce friction in an engine or a machine.

Magnetometer Survey Geological survey identifying sedimentary basins by measuring the magnetic properties of the underlying igneous rock.

Majors Multinational oil companies, which by virtue of size, age, and/or degree of integration, are among the pre-eminent companies in the international petroleum industry.

Marginal Field Oil or gas field whose development depends on whether it will generate enough net income at a given time. It may later become commercial, if conditions change.

Marker Crude Market term referring to any crude oil which is used as a reference for pricing lesser known grades. The term has been used by OPEC to designate Arabian Light (Saudi Arabia's 34 degree API crude) when it served as a pricing benchmark.

MCF The abbreviation for thousand cubic feet, used when describing US natural gas prices. (Derived from the Latin mille, meaning thousand.) MMCF designates million cubic feet.

Methane Odourless inflammable gas which forms an explosive mixture with air.

Methanol Methyl alcohol—a colourless, poisonous liquid with a faint smell—used to mix with petrol to help power vehicles.

Midcontinent Crude Oil Oil produced in Kansas, Oklahoma and North Texas.

Middle Distillates Hydrocarbons that are in the middle range of refinery distillation such as heating oil, diesel fuel and kerosene.

Modules Packages of equipment for installation on a production platform offshore.

Motor Gasoline (Mogas) A complex mixture of relatively volatile hydrocarbons, with or without small quantities of additives, that have been blended to form a fuel suitable for use in spark-ignition engines. The abbreviation Mogas is used to avoid confusion between natural gas and gasoline ("gas").

MR-Cargo Medium range cargo of oil products (25,000 to 30,000 tonnes).

Naphtha A range of distillates covering the heavier end of the gaseous fuel and the lighter end of the kerosene range. A volatile, colourless product used as a paint solvent, cleaning fluid, a feedstock for ethylene and blendstock in gasoline production.

Natural Gas Mixture of light hydrocarbons (predominantly methane), which occur naturally in the Earth's crust and are frequently found in association with oil.

Natural Gas Liquids (NGL) Consists of natural gas, liquid petroleum gases and natural gasoline.

Natural Gasoline A light liquid hydrocarbon mixture recovered from natural gas that is similar to motor gasoline but with a lower octane number.

Netback In common usage netback refers to the value of a crude oil once it has been refined and the products from it sold, taking into account freight and refining costs, e.g. crude traded in a netback deal is sold at a price that reflects the value of the product it yields. It is also a generic term for the net FOB cost after freight charges have been deducted from the CIF price.

Nominations Each month term contract holders submit "nominations" to sellers, telling them how much crude they intend to lift that month. See **Term Customer, Lifting**.

NYMEX New York Mercantile Exchange, which trades heating oil and gasoline futures.

Obligatory Wells Wells drilled in a given area as a condition for receiving an exploration licence.

Octane Number A measure of the resistance of a fuel of pre-ignition ("knock") when burned in an internal combustion engine.

Offtake To load or lift crude.

Off Spec Product that does not meet specifications—referring to either those generally accepted in the trade for a particular product, or to specifications laid down in a contract.

Oil Gasification   Manufacture of gas from oil for use as a fuel.

Oil In Place   An estimated measure of the total amount of oil contained in a reservoir, and as such is a higher figure than that for estimated recoverable reserves.

Oil Patch   A colloquialism referring to areas of the southwest United States such as Texas and Oklahoma where there has been much drilling and production.

Oil Slick   A layer of oil floating on the surface of the sea, generally caused by some sort of accident or spillage, but which is occasionally caused by natural seepage from the ocean floor.

Oil Trap   Hydrocarbon retained by a geological structure and resulting in the formation of an oil field.

Operator   An individual, partnership or corporation that has legal authority to drill wells and undertake production if hydrocarbons are found. The operator coordinates a programme of exploration and development of the licensed area(s) on behalf of its co-licensees (if any).

Organisation of Arab Petroleum Exporting Countries (OAPEC)   Set up in 1968 and headquartered in Kuwait, it is an association separate from the oil price fixing and Vienna-based OPEC. Its members are Algeria, Bahrain, Iraq, Kuwait, Libya, Qatar, Saudi Arabia, Syria, Tunisia, United Arab Emirates and Egypt (currently suspended).

Organisation of Petroleum Exporting Countries (OPEC)   Founded in 1960 and headquartered in Vienna. Its members are Algeria, Ecuador, Gabon, Indonesia, Iran, Iraq, Kuwait, Libya, Nigeria, Qatar, Saudi Arabia, United Arab Emirates and Venezuela. In 1987 it accounted for some 32 per cent of world oil production. It sets an official price for crude oil which may dictate world price levels.

OSP   Official selling price.

Palaeozoic Era   Era of geological time (comprising the Cambrian, Ordovician, Silurian, Devonian, Carboniferous and Permian Periods) which began roughly 600 million years ago and ended roughly 230 million years ago. See **Jurassic** and **Triassic**.

Paper Barrel   A cargo of oil traded for short-term hedging or speculative purposes but not usually physically delivered. See **Wet Barrel**.

Paraffin   Term given in the UK to the top grade of kerosene used in lamps and space heaters.

Participation   Part ownership by a company or government in an oil venture or operation.

Participation Crude Oil	A government's allocation of crude output, usually a percentage of production, taken in some joint ventures between governments and oil companies as payment for granting exploration and development rights.
Pay Zone	Layer of rock in which oil and/or gas is found.
Permeability	The degree to which a rock will allow liquid or gas to pass through it.
Petrochemical	Chemical substance derived from petroleum or natural gas, e.g. ethylene, propylene, benzene and toluene.
Petrodollars	See entry under **Economy, Currency**.
Petroleum	Mixture of hydrocarbons and other organic compounds. It includes crude oil, natural gas liquids, natural gas and their products.
Pig	Object placed in pipeline and propelled by gas or oil flow to clean, clear or check the internal condition of the pipeline.
Plateau Level	Level of peak production reached by an oil or gas field.
Platform	Offshore structure enabling development wells to be drilled. See **Drilling Rig, Drilling Platform** and **Production Platform**.
Plugging	Sealing of well which is no longer, and not likely to be, needed.
Pore Pressure	Original pressure in a rock formation. Porosity is a measure of the amount of gaps or voids in a rock and is normally recorded as a percentage of the overall volume.
Possible Reserves	Oil and/or gas reserves which the best estimates suggest might eventually be recoverable from undrilled or untested structures, but which have not yet been developed.
Posted Price	The price some oil purchasers, especially in the USA, will pay for crude of a certain API gravity from a particular field or area. It has also been the hypothetical price level on which OPEC governments based their "take" from foreign producing companies in the form of taxes and royalties.
Potential Test	Test which provides information on the productive capacity of a well.
Pour Point	For petroleum it is the lowest temperature at which the oil will pour or flow when it is chilled under prescribed conditions.

Primary Recovery	Recovery of oil or gas from a reservoir purely by using the natural pressure in the reservoir to force the oil or gas out.
Probable Reserves	Undeveloped oil and/or gas reserves considered to be recoverable from penetrated formations but lacking information to be classified as proven reserves.
Product Yield	The percentages of gasoline, jet fuel, kerosene, gas oil, distillates, residual fuel oil and other products that a refinery can produce from a 42-US gallon barrel of crude. As a rough guide, the average yield from one barrel is about 50 per cent gasoline, 21 per cent gas oil and distillates, 9 per cent residual fuel oil, 7 per cent jet fuel and kerosene, 7 per cent lubricating oil and 6 per cent other products.
Production Platform	Platform from which development wells are drilled and which carries all the associated processing plant and other equipment needed to maintain a field in production.
Production Sharing Contract	Agreement between an oil firm and a government giving the firm, which often bears all costs, exploration and production rights and the government a share of total output.
Prompt Barrel	Product which will move or become available within three to four days.
Propane	An important raw material in the chemical and plastics industries which is a gas but can be easily converted to a liquid. It is also used as a household fuel.
Prorationing	Regulation of oil and gas production by producing states to conserve natural resources.
Proven Field	Field whose physical extent and estimated reserves have been established.
Proven Reserves	Proven or proved reserves are oil and gas already located and known to be recoverable with existing facilities and present technology and at current cost and price levels.
Recoverable Reserves	Oil/gas known to exist and be economically recoverable. Of the total hydrocarbons in place only a proportion can be ultimately recovered, depending on the permeability of the rock, the properties of the oil for example, and the type of natural drive available. At the extremes between 10 and 80 per cent of the original oil in place can be recovered in the primary phase but the norm is below 30 per cent. Thereafter, depending on the success of secondary recovery techniques the figure can be improved upon, but the final figure for recoverable reserves will only be known once the field is in production. While this often results in an upgrading of the

estimated recoverable reserves, there are many instances where the reverse has been true.

Recovery Factor
Ratio of oil and/or gas reserves which can currently be recovered to estimated total deposits.

Refinery
Plant used to separate the various components present in crude oil and convert them into end-use products or feedstock for other manufacturing processes.

Reserves
See **Dedicated Reserves, Oil In Place, Possible Reserves, Probable Reserves, Proven Reserves** and **Recoverable Reserves**.

Reservoir Rock
Porous and permeable rock, e.g. dolomite, sandstone or limestone, which contains hydrocarbons.

Residual Fuel Oil
Very heavy fuel oils produced from the residue after the fractional distillation process.

Rig
See **Drilling Rig**.

Riser (Pipe)
Wide diameter pipeline linking an offshore platform to a subsea wellhead or spur line.

Royalty
Share of the production or revenue reserved by whoever granted the oil lease or licence.

Saturation Diving
Divers working and living under high pressure for long periods rather than undergoing decompression after every job.

Secondary Recovery
Technique for recovering oil and gas from a reservoir by artificially maintaining or enhancing the reservoir pressure through the injection of gas, water or other substances into the reservoir rock.

Seismic Survey
Survey to establish the structure of underground rock by creating shock waves in the strata and then measuring the reflected signals, i.e. vibrations.

Semi-Submersible Rig
Floating drilling platform that is supported by underwater pontoons.

Shale Oil
Oil extracted from certain kinds of shale deposits. The shale is heated and resulting vapours are condensed and treated to form shale oil or synthetic oil.

Sour Crude
High sulphur content crude oil.

Sour Gas
Gas, either associated or natural, with a high sulphur content.

Specifications
Term referring to the properties of a given crude oil or refined petroleum product, which are "specified" since they often vary widely even within the same grade of product.

Specific Gravity
Ratio of density of a substance at a particular temperature to the density of water at 4 degrees C.

Spot Market
Physical supplies of crude oil or petroleum products sold on a one-time basis, with deals sometimes arranged by brokers.

Spudding In
Starting to drill an oil/gas well by making a hole with a large diameter bit.

Standby Boat
Boat maintaining permanent station near an offshore structure in order to provide support facilities in an emergency.

Step Out Well
A well drilled away from a discovery well to assess the reservoir area.

Stripper Well
An onshore oil well that produces less than 10 barrels per day and is uneconomical to shut down on a temporary basis.

Sub-Sea Wellhead
Wellhead installed on the sea floor and controlled remotely from a platform or floating production facility or from land. See **Wellhead**.

Sweet Crude
Crude oil with a low sulphur content, such as those from North Africa, Nigeria and the North Sea.

Synthetic Natural Gas (SNG)
Gas manufactured from coal or oil that has the same basic chemical composition and burning characteristics as natural gas.

Term Customer
Buyer in long-term contract agreements. Opposite to spot market purchaser.

Term Liftings
Oil lifted under a long-term contract.

Terminal
Onshore installation designed to receive oil and/or gas from a pipeline or from tankers. It is not a refinery.

Tertiary Recovery
Oil or gas recovery from a reservoir in excess of that possible by primary and secondary recovery and requiring special techniques.

Thermal Cracking
This occurs when basic hydrocarbon feedstock is broken down (cracked) to produce light products, through the sole use of heat and pressure, without employing a catalyst.

Throughput
Total volume of raw materials processed by a plant such as an oil refinery in a given period. Also, the total volume of

crude oil and refined products handled by a storage facility or pipeline.

Tight Hole

An exploratory oil well which has been drilled but whose drilling results are withheld by the operator for confidential commercial reasons.

Tonne

The measurement for crude oil in many countries. One tonne of oil is the equivalent to approximately 7.3 or 7.4 barrels of crude. The exact conversion of tonnes into barrels depends on temperature, specific gravity and other physical factors. See **Barrels**. See **Metric Ton** under COMMODITIES.

Town Gas

Locally manufactured gas fuel, originally made from coal.

Triassic Era

Period of geological time starting about 230 million years ago and ending 180 million years ago. See **Jurassic** and **Palaeozoic**.

ULCC (Ultra Large Crude Carrier)

See entry under **Shipping**.

Unitisation

After the owners of oil and/or gas reserves pool their individual interests in return for an interest in the overall unit, this unit is operated by a single company on behalf of the group, thus increasing efficiency.

Uplift

Amount of oil that can be annually recovered from a field before taxes have to be paid.

Viscosity

Measures the resistance of a fluid to motion or flow; as the temperature rises, the viscosity normally decreases.

VLCC (Very Large Crude Carrier)

See entry under SHIPPING.

Volatility

Ease with which a product begins to vaporise. Volatile substances have high vapour pressures, and therefore boil at relatively low temperatures.

Wall Street Refiner

A Wall Street investment firm, which buys or sells crude oil and petroleum products, whether as futures contracts or paper barrels, on a scale similar to that of real refineries. Typically, these investment firms do not own oil refineries and take no actual delivery of the oil.

Water Injection

Process of pumping water into the reservoir rock to maintain pressure.

Wax

Solid hydrocarbon found in certain crude oils. Wax deposits

in pipelines and equipment can cause exploitation and refining problems.

Weather Window   Time in the month or year when weather conditions are suitable, or likely to be so, for various offshore operations, e.g. platform installation.

Well Logging   Comprehensive record of data obtained when drilling a well, providing a very detailed image of the underground rock formation.

Wellhead   Control equipment fitted to the top of a well casing, incorporating outlets, valves, blowout preventer etc.

Wellhead Price   The price of crude, natural gas or condensates as they come from the well.

Wet Barrel   An actual barrel of crude or product already physically in storage at the time of a given transaction, as opposed to a "paper barrel" which appears only as a credit in an accountant's ledger. See **Paper Barrel**.

Well Natural Gas   Natural gas with large amounts of associated liquids. A wet gas may suggest the gas is being recovered from the vicinity of an oil reservoir.

Wild Well   Well which is out of control and blowing fluid or gas from the down hole reservoir.

Wildcat   Exploration well drilled without knowledge of what the underlying rock formation may contain.

Wildcat Appraisal Well   Well drilled with the minimum of preliminary information about the underground formation. Normally used after a wildcat well has shown signs of oil or gas.

Shipping

AA
Always afloat. The charterer accepts the ship will always be afloat during the charter period whether in port or at sea, to avoid damage to the hull.

Abandonment
Used when a ship is abandoned as dangerous or unseaworthy; normally implies the vessel is a total loss.

ABS
American Bureau of Shipping—American ship classification society.

Actual Total Loss
Used in insurance; especially marine insurance, implying complete destruction. It can be presumed if a ship is missing.

Address Commission
Commission paid to the charterer's agent for arranging the loading of a vessel.

Advance Freight
Freight paid in advance. It enables the shipper to endorse the bill of lading with a freight release, and the importer to take immediate delivery.

Affreightment
See **Contract Of Affreightment**.

Afloat
Goods on the high seas en route to their destination. Does not apply to arrivals ready for unloading.

AFRA
Average Freight Rate Assessment. An assessment calculated monthly by the London Tanker Brokers Panel of the average cost of transporting oil in several different sizes of tankers.

AG
Arabian Gulf.

Against All Risks
Insured against all generally accepted risks in marine insurance.

Agency Fee
Charge by a ship's agent or shipowner for services while the ship is in port.

A/H
Ports of Antwerp and Hamburg.

Alongside
Goods delivered alongside a ship for delivery to the dock or lighter from which they can be loaded aboard.

Anchorage
(a) Dues to be paid for anchoring in certain harbours and ports. (b) Place where a ship waits for its berth.

APS
Arrival Pilot Station.

ARA
Antwerp/Rotterdam/Amsterdam (ports).

At And From Marine insurance covering a ship at sea and in port.

ATDONSHINC Anytime day or night Sundays and holidays inclusive.

Backed Note Note authorising a ship's master to take on waterborne goods and evidence that freight changes are covered.

BAF Bunker adjustment factor. A surcharge imposed by shipping conferences to cover bunker fuel price fluctuations.

Bail Bond Bond given to a court to secure the release of an arrested vessel.

Bale Capacity The cubic capacity of a space when the breadth is taken from inside the cargo battens, the depth from the wood ceiling to the underside of the deck beams and the length from inside the bulk head stiffeners or sparring where fitted.

Bale Cargo Goods wrapped in burlap or similar material for shipment overseas.

Ballast Bonus (BB) Lump sum figure paid to cover a voyage in ballast i.e. without cargo.

Baltic Exchange A London freight market engaged in matching cargoes to ships and vice versa and covering both seaborne and air freight. Other activites include grain, soybean meal, potato, meat and freight futures trading. See **Baltic Futures Exchange** under COMMODITIES.

Bareboat Charter Ship charter arranged for a specific period under which the charterer in effect takes control of the vessel, paying all operating and voyage costs.

Barge Flat-bottomed freight boat for canals, rivers and harbours.

Barratry An illegal, fraudulent or negligent act committed by the master or crew to the prejudice of the owner or charterer.

Batten Fitted Pieces of wood fixed above a cargo to keep it in place.

BC British Columbia, or, Bulk Carrier.

Beam Width of ship.

Bends Short for "both ends". The term is normally used when the load and discharge of a vessel is the same, or when a description of the load and discharge is the same, such as "Shex" and "Shinc".

Berth Bill Of Lading Bill of lading issued by the master of a vessel belonging to a regular shipping line.

Berth Terms — Terms under which the shipowner pays loading and discharge costs. Also described as gross terms.

BFI–Baltic Freight Index — An index based on a specified number of dry cargo voyages, each weighted according to its importance in the market and historical data.

B/H — The ports of Bordeaux/Hamburg.

BHF — Bulk harmless fertilisers.

BIFFEX — The Baltic International Freight Futures Exchange Ltd trades dry cargo shipping futures and is one of several markets comprising the Baltic Futures Exchange. See **Baltic Futures Exchange** under COMMODITIES.

Bill Of Lading — Used in foreign trade to describe fully the details of the goods being sent. A marine bill of lading can give the holder the right of possession to goods and acts as a receipt for the goods. In the USA and UK it is a negotiable instrument and a document of title. The shipowner is compelled to release goods to the first presenter of a bill of lading, in the absence of prima facie evidence of fraud.

Bottomry Bond — If a ship's master requires funds urgently to complete a voyage, he can borrow on the security of the ship and cargo via a bottomry bond. Communication with the owner must be impossible, and no other way of raising money, such as using the shipowner's credit, must be available.

Breakbulk — General cargo conventionally stowed as opposed to bulk, unitised or containerised cargo, or goods that have been stripped from containers for forwarding to final destination.

Broken Stowage — Cargo space lost due to packages of uneven shape.

Bunker Fuel — See entry under **Energy**.

BV — Bureau Veritas—French Ship Classification Society.

C and F — Cost and freight. Includes both the cost of the goods and freight charges.

C and F FO — Cost and freight, free out. Includes the cost of the goods, freight charges and unloading. Most grain/sugar is traded on this basis.

CAF — Currency adjustment factor. A charge imposed by shipping conferences to cover currency fluctuations.

CAN — Calcium Ammonium Nitrate.

Cancelling	A date agreed by shipowner and charterer by which time a vessel must be ready to load at latest or the charter may be cancelled.
Cape-Sized Vessels	Bulk carriers and combos of about 100,000 to 150,000 dwt. (Originally these ships were too large for the Suez canal, so they voyaged via the Cape of Good Hope.)
Cargo Preference	Policy whereby a country gives its own ships priority in the ocean carriage of its exports and imports before allowing ships of other countries a share. An agreement to share cargo, normally made within a liner conference, is referred to as cargo sharing. See **Liner Conference**.
Cargo Sharing	See **Cargo Conference**.
CBT	Clean ballast tank.
CFS	Container Freight Station.
CGRT	See **Compensated Gross Registered Tonnage**.
Chartering Agent	A specialised broker engaged in finding cargo space.
Charterparty	Contract under which the charterer has the use of the ship for the carriage of goods for a voyage or a certain time. Such a contract may also act as security for a loan to the shipowner from a bank. The money paid to the owner is known as freight.
Charterparty Assignment	Legal agreement under which the sum paid by the charterer to the shipowner is assigned to a bank as security for a loan to the owner, often for the construction of a vessel.
CHOPT	Charterer's option.
CIF	See entry under GENERAL MARKET TERMS.
Classification Register	Publication issued by a classification society which lists all the ships classed by that society, and in some cases, all other ships over a certain size. See **Lloyd's Register**.
Clean Oil Vessel	Ship employed in carrying refined products. See **Clean (White)** under ENERGY.
Clearance	Volume of goods cleared through a port.
CNR	Charterer not reported.
Combo	Combined carrier. Vessel able to carry ore, oil or bulk cargoes.

Compensated Gross Registered Tonnage (CGRT) — Measurement based on the weight of a standard cargo ship. It is used to calculate actual work involved in building all types of vessels.

Conference Lines — Association of ship owning lines which operate on a given route. Standard tariff rates are fixed and a regular service operated for the mutual benefit of both the merchant trading in that area and the shipowner who runs his line.

Consecutives — A specific number of voyages performed one after another on a single voyage basis for the account of one charterer.

Consignment — Goods shipped by a producer or dealer to an agent on the understanding they will be sold at the best possible price or properly looked after. The shipper retains ownership.

Contract Of Affreightment (COA) — The provision of a certain tonnage capacity to transport bulk cargo during a specific period between two ports or areas at agreed rates.

COP — Custom of port. Relates to customs and practices which have gradually been established for movements in a port, usually concerning loading and discharge.

COW — Crude oil washing.

Cristal — Contract regarding a Supplement to Tanker Liability for Pollution. Provides compensation on a worldwide basis for oil pollution caused by tankers, supplemental to that provided by shipowners. See **TOVALOP**.

Days Purpose — Number of days required by a ship for loading and unloading purposes.

Dead Freight — Paid when a charterer does not provide a full cargo, and the shipowner charges freight for the space which would have been used.

Deadweight — Weight which a vessel is capable of carrying by way of cargo, plus bunkers, stores and fresh water, when loading to the maximum permitted marks. The weight is measured in long tons (2,240 lbs) or tonnes (2,204 lbs).

Demise Charter — Charter of a ship which transfers ownership of the vessel to the charterer for the duration.

Demurrage — Extra charge made by the shipowner if a vessel takes more than the agreed time for loading and discharge.

Dirty (Black) — Crude or unrefined oil.

Dirty Bill Of Lading	Bill of lading which qualifies the goods being carried. Also known as Foul Bill of Lading.
Dirty Oil Vessels	Vessels carrying crude oil, fuel and diesel and some lower grades of oil.
DOP	Dropping Outward Pilot.
Draught	The distances between the keel of a ship and the water surface. A safe draught allows the vessel to negotiate shallow water and prevents it becoming unstable.
Dunnage	Material used to prevent cargo from coming into contact with the ship's metal structure or other cargo, and thereby suffering damage such as sweating, breakage or chaffing. Materials used include boards, matting and burlap.
DWCC	Deadweight cargo capacity.
DWT	Deadweight tons/tonnes. See **Deadweight**.
Dynamic Positioning	When a vessel or drill ship is kept on position by computer-controlled propellers rather than by anchors.
ECSA	East Coast South America.
Ex Quay	Goods available at the quayside.
Ex Ship	Price quoted for goods on arrival at port. It does not include costs of unloading and delivery to the premises of the buyer.
FAC	(a) Fast as can. A vessel will load or discharge as fast as she can take on board or unload. This implies an obligation upon the part of the charterer to supply the cargo as fast as the ship requires it. The term should not be read as obligation to take cargo at a rate which is in excess of the customary daily discharging rate of the port. (b) Forwarding agent's commission.
FAE	Free alongside elevator.
FAS	See entry under GENERAL MARKET TERMS.
FCL	Full Container Load. A fully loaded container which may be in weight or cubic measurement terms; or arrangement whereby a shipper utilises all the space in a container which he packs himself.
FD	Free discharge. The cost of unloading the vessel is paid by the charterer or receiver.
FEU	40 ft equivalent unit. See **TEU**.

FHEX

Fridays and holidays excluded. Refers to unloading and loading which will not be carried out during official holidays nor on Fridays in Islamic countries.

FIO

Free in and out. The cost of loading and unloading is borne by the charterer, shipper or receiver, not by the shipowner.

Fleet Policy

Marine insurance policy covering vessels operated by a single ownership or management.

Flush Tweendecker

Tweendecker whose hatches are level with the flooring so that vehicles can move over the floor freely. See **Tweendecker**.

FOR

See **Free On Rail**.

FOW

First open water. Usually refers to start of navigation after the winter freeze, especially in the Great Lakes and St Lawrence Seaway.

FR

Full range of ports.

Free In And Out

See **FIO**.

Free On Board

See **FOB** under GENERAL MARKET TERMS.

Free On Rail (FOR)

Price of goods which includes the cost of moving them to a railhead for shipment. Free On Truck (FOT) is a similar term for road transport.

Free Port

Coastal or inland port treated as being outside the customs territory of the host state. Goods can be manufacturered, processed and stored in the port without payment of customs duties and subsequently exported. Sometimes called a Free Trade Zone.

Freeboard

Distance between waterline and ship's main deck.

Freight

(a) Sum or fee paid for chartering a ship, or carrying its cargo. (b) Cargo transported by land, sea or air.

FWAD

Fresh water arrival draft.

Geared

Vessel which has heavy lifts and/or cranes. Note: gearless applies to a ship with little or no means for loading and unloading cargo.

General Average Loss

Marine insurance term for loss at sea as the result of a deliberate act intended to save the ship as a whole, or at least part of the cargo. Jettisoning burning cargo to save the rest of the ship is such a loss, which is shared between the owners of the cargo and the shipowner.

GCBS	General Council of British Shipping.
GL	Great Lakes.
GLR	German Liberty Replacement. See **Liberty Type Vessel**.
Grain Fitted	The vessel has fittings, cargo battens and necessary timber to prevent shifting of grain cargo during voyage.
Gross Registered Tonnage (GRT)	Total enclosed capacity in a ship in units of 100 cubic feet, less certain exempted spaces.
Gross Terms	See **Berth Terms**.
Handysize	Refers in UK to vessels around 15,000 to 25,000 dwt.
HG	Heavy grains i.e. wheat, maize and rye.
HHDW	Handy heavy deadweight for highly compacted scrap metal.
H/L	Heavy lift. A unit of cargo which cannot be lifted by the normal ship's gear.
HR	Hampton Roads: the area on the US East Coast from which most US coal is exported.
HSS	Heavy grains, sorghums and soyas.
Hull Insurance	Insurance of a ship together with liabilities arising from collision etc.
Hypothecation	Letter of hypothecation allows a shipper to borrow from a bank using the vessel as security, but without giving the bank ownership of the security. See entry under LENDING.
IACS	International Association of Classification Societies.
ICS	International Chamber of Shipping.
ILA	International Longshoremen's Association.
IMIF	International Maritime Industries Forum.
IMO	International Maritime Organisation.
Inert Gas System (IGS)	Used on oil tankers with tanks being filled with inert (non combustible) gas so as to prevent explosions.
Inmarsat	The International Maritime Satellite Organisation. It operates a system of satellites providing telephone, telex, data and facsimile, as well as distress and safety communications services, to the shipping and offshore industries.

Intercargo	International Association of Dry Cargo Shipowners.
Intermodal	Carriage by different modes of transport i.e. road, rail, sea, aircraft. See **Multimodal**.
Intertanko	International Association of Independent Tanker Owners.
ISF	International Shipping Federation.
ITF	International Transport Workers Federation. Ships' crews have to be members of the federation if the ships go to certain countries including Finland, Sweden, Australia and France.
IWL	Institute Warranty Limits. Refers to areas where ships can sail without hazards such as ice, icebergs etc.
Jason Clause	Marine insurance term for risks which could not be discovered even if considerable care taken.
Jettison	Throw goods overboard to lighten a vessel.
Knot	A measurement of speed. One nautical mile equals 6,080 feet per hour.
Lakehead	Ports of Duluth, Superior and Thunder Bay in the Great Lakes.
Lakes Fitted	Vessel equipped to move through the Great Lakes with fenders fitted for passing through locks. It must not be more than 75 feet in width.
Lay Barge	See entry under ENERGY.
Lay Days	Specific period in days during which a ship must have arrived and be ready for loading operations under a charterparty.
Lay Time	Maximum period during which a charterer can use a vessel for the purpose of loading and unloading cargoes without incurring financial liability known as demurrage.
Lay Up	To withdraw a vessel from trading and moor it semi-permanently at a specific location.
LCL	Less than (full) Container Load. A consignment of cargo which does not fill a shipping container, grouped with other consignments for the same destination.
L/D	Load/discharge.
LG	Light grains (barley and oats).

Liberty Type Vessels	Built by the USA during World War II and mostly multi-purpose cargo ships of about 15,000 dwt. They were tweendeckers. By the mid 1960s most had come to the end of their useful life and various countries started building Liberty replacements. The UK built SD 14s which it also had constructed under licence in Greece and Brazil. The Japanese built Freedom type vessels, and German Liberty Replacements were also built. These were all around 15,000 dwt. Some other types of replacement vessels have been constructed in various countries with sizes ranging from about 15,000 dwt to 22,000 dwt. These include the Santa Fe type vessels built in Spain of around 21,000 dwt.
Light Displacement Tonnes	Weight of a ship's hull, machinery, equipment and spares. This is often the basis on which ships are paid for when purchased for scrapping. The difference between the loaded displacement and light displacement is the ship's **Deadweight**.
Lighter	Boat, usually flat-bottomed, used for loading and unloading those ships not brought to wharf.
Lighterage	Price paid for loading or unloading ships by lighters or barges.
Lightweight Tons (LWT)	Weight of steel in a ship, usually quoted when a ship is sold for scrap, when the price is given in dollars per light ton.
Liner Conference	Voluntary organisation in which a number of shipowners—often of different nationality—offer regular services to a series of ports on a given sea route on conditions agreed by members.
Liner Discharge	Shipowner pays for unloading and stevedores' wages.
Liner Service	Service provided by a shipping company whereby cargo-carrying ships are operated between ports on a regular basis. The freight rates, which are charged, are based on the shipping company's tariff or, if the company is a member of a liner conference, the tariff of that conference.
Liner Terms	Owner is responsible for arranging and paying for loading and discharging of ship.
Lloyd's Register	Published in London, this is an annual alphabetical list of commercial vessels of more than 100 tons on a worldwide basis classified according to seaworthiness. As a classification society, Lloyd's formulates rules for the building of vessels and assigns classes to them when its rules have been followed.
LOA	Length overall of a vessel.

Manifest　　Detailed list of cargo carried aboard a vessel or plane.

Marpol　　A convention aimed at preventing marine pollution from ships and adopted by the International Maritime Organisation.

MBT　　Motor blocks and turnings.

MOL　　More or less.

MOP　　Muriate of Potash.

Multimodal　　A transport service offering more than one transport mode. See **Intermodal**.

Nautical Mile　　Varies from 6,045.93 ft on the Equator to 6,107.98 ft in latitude 90 degrees. A mean nautical mile is 6,076.91 ft.

NB　　Newly built vessel.

Net Registered Tonnage (NRT)　　This is the part of a ship's gross registered tonnage considered for cargo. It is the gross tonnage less the machinery, boiler and bunker, crew and stores space.

Newbuilding　　Newly built ship.

NKK　　Nippon Kaiji Kyokai—Japanese Ship Classification Society.

NOLA　　New Orleans.

Non O/A　　Not over age. This usually means when a charterer does not want a vessel more than 15 years old.

OBO　　Ore/bulk/oil carrier.

O/O　　Ore/oil carrier.

Over Age　　A vessel more than 15 years old, although occasionally it can refer to a vessel of more than 20 years. Additional insurance is charged on an over age vessel.

Overage　　Extra cargo which a tanker may have the option to carry in addition to a part cargo already fixed.

P and I Club　　Protection and Indemnity Club. Refers to the various associations of shipping companies which have been formed to provide protection against risks not covered by ordinary marine insurance.

Pallion Vessel　　A vessel of around 17,000 long dwt built at the Pallion shipyard in the UK.

Panamax	A size of ship measured by whether it is capable of transiting the Panama Canal. Usually below about 65,000 dwt.
Part Cargo (PC)	Acceptance by a shipowner of a charter under which the ship will not be fully loaded and unused space is not paid for.
Particular Average Loss	Damage caused to a particular cargo, with the loss borne by the insurers of that cargo alone.
PG	Persian Gulf.
PH	Per hatch. Loading or discharging is often given as so many tons per hatch day (phd).
Plimsoll Line	Water level on British registered vessels which indicates the maximum permitted loading level.
PMO	Passing Muscat outbound. Muscat is a port in the Sultanate of Oman.
PP	Picked (selected) ports.
Prolerised Scrap	Scrap metal which has been broken up.
Prompt	Term applied to a vessel able to arrive at a required loading port within a few days.
PWH	Per working hatch.
Reefer	Refrigerated cargo ship.
Relet	Term for a ship already on period commitment which is made available for a single voyage or period to a further charterer.
RNR	Rate not reported.
RO/RO	Roll on/roll off ships, which allow containers to be driven on and off without the use of cranes.
R/V	Round voyage.
Salvage	Reward for saving all or part of a ship or cargo from shipwreck.
Santa Fe Type Vessel	See **Liberty Type Vessel**.
SBM	Soybean meal.
SBT	Segregated ballast tanks.

Shelterdeck Vessel which has a higher than normal superstructure above the main deck of the vessel. To be a true shelterdeck ship, a tonnage opening should be fitted and the end of the deck left unclosed. When a cargo is carried in this space, the space is calculated in the ship's tonnage figures. If the space is open and unused, it is excluded from tonnage figures and no dues are charged on this space.

SHEX Sundays and holidays exempted. SSHEX adds Saturdays to the definition.

SHINC Sundays and holidays included. SSHINC adds Saturdays.

Shipbroker Agent for the shipowner or shipping company handling cargo space, insurance, freight, passengers, ship chartering.

Shipper Consignor of cargo, often an exporter.

Shipping Register See **Classification Register** and **Lloyd's Register**.

Slot Charter The chartering of a ship by a fleet operator for a specific voyage when none of the ships in the fleet is available.

SOLAS (a) System under which tweendeck vessels can load bulk grains without fittings or bags while ensuring cargo stability. (b) The international convention for the Safety of Life at Sea.

Spot Term for a ship available for charter in the immediate vicinity of a charterer's requirements for tonnage. See entry under GENERAL MARKET TERMS.

Spout Trimmed (SPT) A vessel loaded with a bulk cargo trimmed or levelled off. Commodities like grains are often spout trimmed, which means they are loaded by a spout or chute which ensures level loading.

STL St Lawrence.

Stem Subject to availability of cargo.

Stowed Cargo packed and secured for a voyage.

Subject Stem A vessel that has been chartered for business but without confirmation that the cargo will be available on time.

SWAD Salt water arrival draft.

T/A Transatlantic.

TBN To be nominated.

Territorial Waters	The United Nations Law of the Sea Convention adopted in April 1982 establishes a 12 nautical mile territorial sea zone, and a 200 nautical mile exclusive economic zone for coastal states. The convention has to be ratified by participating states.
TEU	Twenty Foot Equivalent Units. The area of a container ship is often given in TEUs.
Timecharter	Ship charter arranged for a fixed period. Payment is either in dollars per deadweight ton per month or dollars daily, but it excludes voyage costs. The charterer has the use of the vessel with the shipowner supplying the crew and provisions.
Tonnage	See **Deadweight, Gross Registered Tonnage, Lightweight Tons** and **Net Registered Tonnage**.
TOVALOP	Tanker Owners Voluntary Agreement on Liability for Oil Pollution. A means by which tanker owners provide compensation on a worldwide basis for pollution damage and cleanup costs arising from oil spills from their tankers. See **Cristal**.
Tramco Vessel	Multi-purpose cargo ship of 7,000 to 10,000 dwt built in West Germany.
Tramp Vessel	Vessel engaged in casual trade, or upon charter party fixtures, each of which operates as a separate voyage and does not constitute part of a regular service.
Trimmed	Levelling of a cargo after loading.
Tweendecker	A ship with two decks of which the upper one is the main deck.
ULCC	Ultra large crude carrier. To London brokers this generally means a crude oil tanker of 320,0000 long deadweight tons or above. See **VLCC**.
Ullage	Distance between top of cargo and the hatches.
USAC	US Atlantic Coast.
USG	US Gulf ports.
USNH	USA north of Hatteras. Hatteras is a cape in North Carolina on the USA Atlantic Coast and USNH covers ports such as New York, Boston, Philadelphia, Baltimore, Norfolk, Newport News and Portland, Maine. Also referred to as US Northern Range.

USNP   US North Pacific ports.

USSH   US ports south of Hatteras.

VGO   Vacuum gas oil.

VLCC   Very large crude carrier. Tanker capable of carrying large amounts of crude oil. Usually for London brokers a minimum of 160,000 long dwt would be necessary to qualify a vessel as a VLCC. See **ULCC**.

Voyage Charter   Ship charter arranged to carry a cargo on a single voyage between specified ports or areas. Payment, usually on either a cargo ton basis or on a cubic capacity basis, includes voyage costs.

Voyage Costs   Vessel costs comprising bunkers, port and canal charges.

Voyage Policy   Marine insurance policy issued for one particular voyage only.

Waiver Clause   In marine insurance a provision enabling either party to take steps to reduce the impact of a loss without prejudice.

War Risk   Risk a shipper may encounter as a consequence of war in despatching a specified consignment.

WCSA   West Coast South America.

Worldscale (WS)   The Worldwide Tanker Nominal Freight Scale. A freight index designed to express tanker rates irrespective of vessel size and route, in terms of the costing of a standard vessel. It is customary to negotiate levels of freight for tankers expressed as a percentage of the Worldscale freight rates which are given in dollars. Thus Worldscale 100 means that the rate is as published by the Worldscale Association (NYC) Inc in New York and by the Worldscale Association (London) Ltd. Worldscale 200 would mean double the published rate.

    A new scale is scheduled to take effect from January 1989, incorporating various changes in the worldscale formula. The two Worldscale Associations will henceforth make one yearly revision to the rate on January 1 (instead of half-yearly changes), reflecting fluctuations in bunker prices and port costs.

WWD   Weather working days. This usually qualifies "Shex" or "Shinc" and means the exclusion of time lost through bad weather.

Abbreviations and Acronyms

FAO 131
FAQ 131
FAS 7, 171
FAZ 100
FCIA 66
FCL 171
FCOJ 139
FD 171
FDIC 64
FECOM 31, 32
FEFAC 131
FELABAN 33
FEOGA 130
FERC 153
FEU 171
FHEX 172
FHLB 64
FIBOR 64
FIFO 100
FIMBRA 100
FIO 172
FIRS 131
FNMA 64
FOB 8, 158
FOMC 64
FOR 172
FORMA 132
FOT 172
FOW 172
FOX 137
FR 172
FRA 66
FRCD 65
FRN 65
FTC 100
FWAD 172

G-5 35, 36
G-7 35, 36
G-10 35, 36
GAB 35, 66
GATT 35, 139
GCBS 173
GDP 36
GEPLACEA 133
GL 173
GLR 173
GNMA 67

GNP 36
GPM 134
GRT 173
GSA 133
GSP 35
GTC 9

HFCS 134, 135
HG 134, 173
HHDW 173
HIBOR 68
H/L 173
HR 173
HSS 173

IAA 134
IACO 134
IACS 173
IADB 37, 38
IBC 134
IBEC 37
IBF 104
IBRD 86
ICA 134
ICC 38
ICCA 134
ICCH 135
ICCO 134
ICO 134
ICS 173
IDA 70
IEA 155
IFC 70
IGS 173
ILA 173
ILO 37
ILZSG 135
IMC 37
IMF 37, 39, 70, 123
IMIF 173
IMM 37
IMO 173
IMRO 104
Inmarsat 173
INRA 135
INRO 135
Intercargo 174

Intertanko 174
IP 155
IPE 137, 155
IRSG 135
ISA 135
ISF 174
ISO 135
ITA 135
ITC 135
ITF 174
ITSG 135
IWA 135
IWC 135
IWCC 135
IWL 174

LACPI 71
LBO 104
LCE 137
LCL 174
L/D 174
LDC 41
LG 174
LGFM 122
LIBID 71
LIBOR 71
LIFFE 41
LIFO 100, 105
LIMEAN 71
LME 142
LMFE 122
LNG 156
LOA 175
LOOP 157
LPFA 122
LPG 157
LUXIBOR 72
LWT 175
LYON 86

M0 42
M1 42
M2 42
M3 42
M4 42
M5 42
MATIF 41